D0998245

BIG
FEELINGS

BIG
FEELINGS

How to Be Okay When
Things Are Not Okay

Liz Fosslien & Mollie West Duffy

ILLUSTRATIONS BY LIZ FOSSLIEN

PORTFOLIO / PENGUIN

Portfolio / Penguin
An imprint of Penguin Random House LLC
penguinrandomhouse.com

Text copyright © 2022 by Liz Fosslien and Mollie West Duffy
Illustrations copyright © 2022 by Liz Fosslien

Penguin supports copyright. Copyright fuels creativity, encourages diverse voices, promotes free speech, and creates a vibrant culture. Thank you for buying an authorized edition of this book and for complying with copyright laws by not reproducing, scanning, or distributing any part of it in any form without permission. You are supporting writers and allowing Penguin to continue to publish books for every reader.

Most Portfolio books are available at a discount when purchased in quantity for sales promotions or corporate use. Special editions, which include personalized covers, excerpts, and corporate imprints, can be created when purchased in large quantities. For more information, please call (212) 572-2232 or email specialmarkets@penguinrandomhouse.com. Your local bookstore can also assist with discounted bulk purchases using the Penguin Random House corporate Business-to-Business program. For assistance in locating a participating retailer, email B2B@penguinrandomhouse.com.

Some illustrations appeared previously on the illustrator's Instagram.

ISBN 9780593418239 (hardcover)
ISBN 9780593418246 (ebook)

Printed in the United States of America
3rd Printing

Book design by Cassandra Garruzzo Mueller

To our readers, who shared their Big Feelings with us

CONTENTS

Introduction

This book almost didn't happen.

We initially pitched the idea for this book in January 2020. Our first book, *No Hard Feelings: The Secret Power of Embracing Emotions at Work*, had been published in February 2019, but in the intervening months, we'd found ourselves struggling with some very hard feelings of our own in both work and life.

Liz's father-in-law was losing his ten-year battle with recurrent cancer, and she had just switched to a new, more stressful role within her company. Mollie had moved across the country and felt isolated as the only person on her team working remotely (pre-COVID). We were also both facing health issues: Liz had wrist and neck aches so severe she feared she would have to abandon her computer-heavy career, and Mollie was in the throes of chronic pain that triggered a long, deep depression and, at times, suicidal thoughts.

And yet, who were we to be depressed or anxious? We had health insurance, we'd just published a bestselling book together, and we were both in stable relationships. We were lucky. So we did everything we could to pull ourselves up off the ground. Relying on the six years we had spent researching emotions and how they impact our lives, we each tried to cope.

But we still felt pummeled by emotions. At times, our efforts even seemed to backfire. Liz's anxiety spiked on no-devices Saturdays. All she could think about were the important emails she might be missing and how overwhelming her inbox would be when she looked at it again. And when Mollie saw the details of her chronic pain written out in her journal, she felt even more hopeless.

We knew we weren't the only ones who had ever struggled, and we wanted to find out what had worked for other people. And so we had the idea to write a book about how to navigate hard feelings. Big feelings.

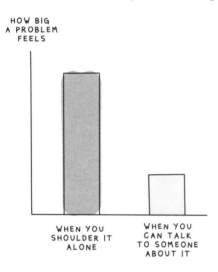

HOW BIG
A PROBLEM
FEELS

WHEN YOU
SHOULDER IT
ALONE

WHEN YOU
CAN TALK
TO SOMEONE
ABOUT IT

When we first told our publishers about the idea, they were skeptical. "Who would this book be for?" our editor asked. "And do they want to talk about difficult emotions?" Then the COVID pandemic hit, and it became clear that a whole lot of people were grappling with big feelings—and looking not only for relief but for recognition. In June 2020, our editor called back: "Remember your idea for a book about difficult emotions? Well, forget what we said. We're in."

As the pandemic raged on, we continued what we'd been doing: leading corporate workshops on emotions at work (now virtually). We noticed that participants were asking different questions: instead of seeking advice on how to have a good one-on-one meeting with their managers, people wanted to know what to do when their lives had been upended. "Half of my team got laid off last week," one woman emailed us after a session. "I feel immense survivor's guilt. I'm also now doing the work of three people. I wake up in the mornings already exhausted. What can I do to feel better?"

Everyone was terrified, for themselves and their loved ones. People asked about ways to handle a mixture of loss, anger, and burnout that stung so bitterly it was hard to process. They wanted advice on how to cope when their daily existence had been transformed by big feelings. All of a sudden, everyone was talking about these difficult feelings, at home and at work (which, for many people, had become the same place).

The shame and secrecy around difficult emotions have certainly lessened in the last few decades, but these stigmas are still a major force in modern culture. Big feelings can't be eliminated; they are ever present in spite of our best intentions to dispel them. Part of being "okay" is learning to live with them rather than trying to get rid of them. Another part is acknowledging them out loud, since silence makes them so much worse.

Honestly, we wrote this book to convince ourselves that we would be okay. We wanted to open up about our struggles in the hope that others would do the same, and that maybe we all could learn something from each other. We're here to say you're not alone, and also to help you figure out how to cope with your big feelings. We wish working through uncomfortable emotions was as easy as reading through a list of affirmations or scheduling a walk with a friend. That would be a short and simple book. But this is going to be messier and more complicated, and we sometimes cried while we wrote it. But that's okay! So. Deep breath. Here we go.

. . .

This is a book about what we call *big feelings*: uncertainty, comparison, anger, burnout, perfectionism, despair, and regret. These seven emotions came up over and over in our conversations with others and are particularly salient in the modern world. We'll also address grief and shame, although not in as much depth, since there are already excellent books that tackle these topics (see "Resources on shame and guilt" on page 235 and "Resources on grief" on pages 236–37).

We started by interviewing psychologists, therapists, and academics on how to navigate difficult emotions. In addition, we spoke with hundreds of people who had read our first book or who followed us on social media. We were struck by the range of responses and by the fact that, across demographic differences like cultural background, race, gender, and sexuality, everyone seemed to say a

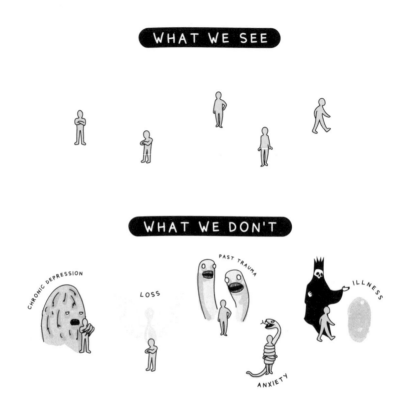

version of the same thing: In today's world, we bump into difficult emotions all the time. And when we do, we often feel stuck, ashamed, and isolated. We have never learned to acknowledge unpleasant feelings, let alone effectively understand and harness them.

So before we dive into specific big feelings, we want to bust three pervasive and harmful myths about them.

The first: Big feelings are "negative." Starting at a young age, most of us are taught that feeling bad is bad. In the spring of 2021, as part of our research for this book, we invited readers to take a survey about their emotional experiences. More than 1,500 people responded, and 97 percent said they have heard big feelings described as "bad" or "negative."

While big feelings are uncomfortable—at times they can even feel unbearable—they aren't inherently positive or negative. When we take the time to understand them, big feelings like anger and regret can serve us. Anger can fuel us to advocate for what matters. And regret can provide us with insight into how to craft a more meaningful life.

STEPS TOWARD HEALING IT

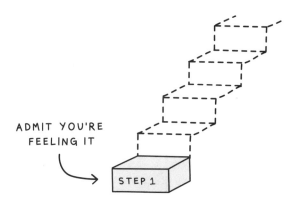

ADMIT YOU'RE FEELING IT

STEP 1

When we change the way we relate to big feelings, we take away some of their destructive power. Research shows that when we acknowledge and accept what we feel during challenging moments, we start to feel better. As a *Washington Post* headline put it, FEELING BAD ABOUT FEELING BAD CAN MAKE YOU FEEL REALLY, REALLY BAD.[1]

The second: You should be strong enough to think your way out of difficult emotions. How many times has someone told you, "Just focus on the positive!" or "Cheer up!"? "This relentless focus on individual effort, and denial that circumstances matter to happiness, has an ideological flavor to it," writes journalist Ruth Whippman in her book *America the Anxious*.[2] "And perhaps this philosophical bent isn't surprising, given the highly conservative nature of the key financial backers of the academic positive psychology movement."

Thinking different thoughts doesn't guarantee that you'll feel different. Life is hard. If we live long enough, we'll watch some of our loved ones die. We'll experience physical pain, and we'll have to endure immensely challenging situations. In those cases, you might fall apart for a bit, or have to leave an unhealthy situation, or seek professional help. That's all okay.

It's also impossible to talk about big feelings without acknowledging that structural forces matter. A lot. If you work in a sexist or racist environment, your mental health will suffer. If your boss constantly demands that you do more and you can't afford to quit your job, you're far more likely to burn out. University of Pennsylvania psychologist Dr. James Coyne puts it more bluntly: "Positive psychology is mainly for rich white people."[3]

And the third: You are the only one who experiences big feelings. In our 2021 survey, 99 percent of people shared that they had struggled with a big feeling over the past month, the most common being uncertainty, burnout, and perfectionism. Reasons ranged from "Tight timelines and overwork" to "Looking up other people's salaries on Glassdoor" to "Constantly doing" to "Others relying on me."

When we keep everything we're feeling bottled up, we suffer in silence—and miss out on the chance to connect with others and to let them support us.

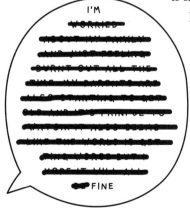

We (Liz and Mollie) are encouraged to see that this is slowly changing: over the past few years, celebrities like rapper Bad Bunny and tennis player Naomi Osaka have openly talked about struggles with anxiety and depression, and companies like LinkedIn and Bumble have given their entire workforce paid time off to help combat burnout. Beginning in 2020, the pandemic forced conversations about mental health that we encourage everyone to continue.

. . .

By now, we've (hopefully) convinced you that it's okay to feel big feelings. We're not going to patronize you by saying, "Strike a pose and take four deep breaths. That should fix everything!" Instead, we're going to lay out a set of strategies intended to help you regain a sense of control and hope when you need it most.

MOOD

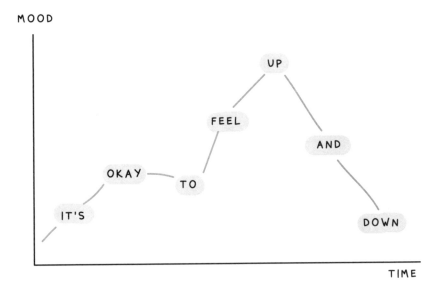

TIME

We distinguish among the seven big feelings—though they usually don't show up in isolation—because it's useful to know how to handle each one. That way, when you find yourself flooded by emotion, you'll be better able to grab exactly what you need from your emotional toolbox. Psychologists call getting specific about what you're feeling *emotional granularity,* and it's the first step in navigating big feelings. A large body of research shows that the ability to pinpoint what we're feeling improves our well-being, physical health, and life satisfaction.

So here are our promises to you. This book will do the following:

- **Carefully examine the seven big feelings of the modern world:** uncertainty, comparison, anger, burnout, perfectionism, despair, and regret.
- **Give you tools to better sit with these emotions,** learn from them, and start the recovery process.
- **Throw out the idea of a one-size-fits-all solution.** Instead, we'll offer you a range of advice, so you can figure out what works for you.
- **Detail our own experiences and share stories** from a wide range of people in order to normalize big feelings.
- **Not trivialize the impact of structural forces.**
- **Help you understand what purpose these emotions serve** and effectively communicate your feelings to others.
- **Empower you to offer support to someone** in your life who might be experiencing a big feeling.

The aim of this book is to be broadly useful without glossing over the ways our emotions are impacted by our societal roles and identities. While we (Liz and Mollie) have different emotions and emotional tendencies, we are both white American women in our early thirties who almost certainly have blind spots. We've balanced our own experiences with stories from a wide range of

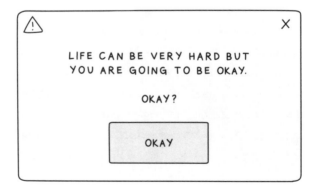

LIFE CAN BE VERY HARD BUT
YOU ARE GOING TO BE OKAY.

OKAY?

OKAY

readers both to represent as many experiences as possible and to show that elements of big feelings are far more common than we might initially believe.

Our hope is that you find tips and tales that resonate with you and that make experiencing big feelings less lonely. "There are two kinds of people who don't experience painful emotions such as anxiety or disappointment, sadness, envy," writes psychologist Tal Ben-Shahar. "The psychopaths and the dead."[4]

BIG
FEELINGS

CHAPTER 1

Uncertainty

Everything's great, and I'm okay.
Everything sucks, and I'm okay.

Jerry Colonna

LIZ: *The first headache hit like a jackhammer. I stumbled toward the bathroom, dizzy and gagging.*

A week later, the second sent me to the emergency room. After a barrage of blood draws and scans, the doctors ruled out a list of life-threatening issues—pulmonary embolism, brain aneurysm, tumor—and categorized me as a medical mystery.

Searching for a diagnosis is excruciating. "Don't worry until you have something to worry about," a coworker told me. But I worried all the time. I yo-yoed between imagining the worst possible outcome and feeling like a drama queen. Was I dying? Or was it absolutely nothing?

That was my life for months. I shuttled between neurologists; ear, nose, and throat specialists; and ophthalmologists. One neurologist gave me thirty-six injections of Botox in my head, shoulders, and back to prevent neurotransmitters from sending pain signals to my brain. An ophthalmologist thought the muscles around my eyes might be in-flamed, and prescribed steroid medication that skyrocketed my blood pressure and made my cheeks flush a dark pink.

Then an internist suggested that I had an atypical case of migraines and put me on a high dosage of Topamax, an antiepileptic drug. The clanging in my skull finally quieted, but the side effects that popped up left me just as out of sorts. My emotions exploded. One afternoon, I stepped onto the L train in Chicago and into the clutches of the worst panic attack I've ever experienced. I clung to a ceiling pole. When the doors opened again, I crawled out onto the Merchandise

Mart platform and forced one foot in front of the other until I was finally back at my apartment. I spent the rest of the day in bed, shaken and ashamed.

In the morning, I emptied the pill bottle into the toilet. I was done with Topamax.

I didn't know that it can be life-threatening to stop prescription medication cold turkey.

At four o'clock the next afternoon, my heart lurched. I managed to make it to the lobby of my apartment building before I lost consciousness. When I came to, I was strapped to a gurney in the back of an ambulance. A nurse's face swam before my eyes. She told me my parents were on their way.

"Am I going to die?" I felt the back of my neck prickle in terror as darkness clouded my vision again.

The nurse looked at the jagged line displayed on a nearby monitor. "I don't know."

"I don't want to die before my mom gets here," I tried to tell her, but I couldn't move my mouth anymore. Then everything went black.

• • •

This is a period of radical uncertainty, [by] an order of magnitude greater than anything we're used to," said Columbia University historian Adam Tooze in April 2020.[1] That October, a *New York Times* headline announced, AWAKE AT 3 A.M.? WE ARE TOO.[2] The same year, the most popular *Harvard Business Review* articles were about how to navigate turbulent times and grieve the loss of a guaranteed future.

As millennials—"the new lost generation," according to *The Atlantic*[3]—we (Liz and Mollie) have lived through three major economic recessions, have quarantined for more than a year during a global pandemic and a devastating wildfire season in California, and view 401(k) matching (let alone pensions) as a

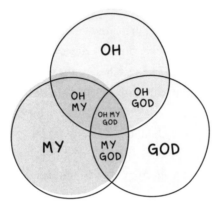

relic. We consider ourselves to be among the fortunate, and even we felt over-whelmed by uncertainty.

Psychologists who study stress have identified three primary factors that make us feel awful: a lack of control, unpredictability, and the perception that things are getting worse.[4] In other words: uncertainty.

In this chapter, we'll deconstruct uncertainty and the emotion at its core: anxiety.[5] To clarify definitions before we continue:

- **Anxiety** is general unease because of an uncertain outcome. We feel anxious when we aren't sure how larger forces will interfere with our lives.
- **Fear** is when we believe that something specific will happen (like tripping over your words during an important presentation, or a loved one dying).

We'll start by walking through three common myths around uncertainty and the anxiety it causes and then offer a few ways to find solid footing even when the world moves beneath you.

MYTHS ABOUT UNCERTAINTY

Myth #1: Certainty is attainable

While sheltering in place during the first few weeks of the pandemic, we felt that we were living through a period of unprecedented uncertainty. (We weren't alone: Google searches for the word "unprecedented" spiked to, well, unprecedented highs in March 2020.[6]) But the level of uncertainty during the Cuban Missile Crisis or World War I or even the bubonic plague was just as great, if not much greater, than it is today.

Life can change in an instant. At age thirty-three, Liz's CrossFit-loving, teetotaling friend developed a sharp pain in his ankle. Three weeks later, he was diagnosed with bone cancer, and a week after that his right leg was amputated. Or take Liz herself, who decided to buy a treat at Berkeley Bowl, a local grocery store, on her way home from a particularly draining day at work. While beelining through the produce section, she bumped into a friend-of-a-friend she had met once years ago. He suggested they grab coffee together sometime. Five years later, she married him.

We tend to be too confident about our ability to predict the future. Behavioral scientists have shown that we're overly optimistic about things we want to happen, we notice immediate changes but tend to overlook longer-term shifts, and we overemphasize the importance of new information that fits into our existing beliefs. If you *really* want to travel to Paris, you'll probably see flight prices going down as a sign but then shrug and ignore it if your hotel stay suddenly becomes more expensive. The track record of "expert" forecasters (think economists and meteorologists) is so dismal that some claim that being an expert in something actually makes you worse at predicting the future than if you were a generalist.[7]

The ancient teachings of Buddhism center on this fundamental problem. "We can try to control the uncontrollable by looking for security and predictability," writes Buddhist teacher Pema Chödrön, "always hoping to be comfortable and safe. But the truth is that we can never avoid uncertainty. This not-knowing is part of the adventure."[8] And precisely what makes us anxious.

Myth #2: Anxiety accurately reflects risk

There's often a mismatch between how stressed we *feel* about something happening and the likelihood that that thing will happen. In an experiment, researchers told one group of people they had a 99 percent chance of receiving a painful (but safe) electric shock and told the other group they had a 1 percent chance.[9] Surprisingly, the two groups were willing to pay about the same amount of money to avoid the shock. In other words, the *likelihood* of getting hurt didn't affect people's *anxiety* about getting hurt—or what they would do to avoid the scenario.

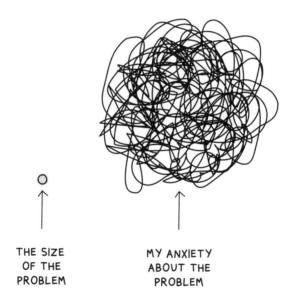

THE SIZE
OF THE
PROBLEM

MY ANXIETY
ABOUT THE
PROBLEM

The more uncertainty we face, the worse we feel. When the risk level of a decision is unknown, brain activity spikes in the area that processes emotions.[10]

Research even shows we'd rather be absolutely sure that something bad is going to happen than deal with ambiguity.[11] Scientists found that people who had a 50 percent chance of receiving an electric shock were *three times* as stressed as people who had a 90 percent chance of getting the shock.[12] (Seems 100 percent certain that uncertainty researchers love delivering electric shocks.)

If we know what the bad thing is, we can plan for it. But when we don't know what's going to happen, we spiral. "I knew for a long time that I had to leave," reader Carmen told us after finally quitting a job that had made her miserable. "But I was so anxious about having to figure out my next steps that I chose unhappiness over uncertainty for *four* years."

So while it's normal to fret in the face of uncertainty, your emotional reaction might be disproportionate to reality. Not knowing is the worst. But it can be useful to say to yourself, "The fact that I'm worried about the future doesn't guarantee that the future will be bad." Ahead of her wedding, reader Marcie had trouble sleeping. "I'm bad with change and get nervous ahead of any big event," she told us. But Marcie, who has now been happily married for twenty-five years, realized, "My insomnia wasn't about me doubting my relationship."

Myth #3: You just need to be more resilient

Over the past few years, "resilience" has popped up everywhere as the answer to everything. Having a hard time because of a toxic environment? Just be resilient. Struggling to homeschool your kids while working fifty-hour weeks during a global pandemic? Try some resilience.

Resilience, or the ability to withstand hardship and bounce back from difficult events, *is* useful. But too often it's presented in a way that overlooks systemic problems and instead encourages individuals to grin and bear whatever tough stuff comes their way. In an article titled "Smile! You've Got Cancer," author Barbara Ehrenreich writes, "There is no kind of problem or obstacle for which positive thinking or a positive attitude has not been proposed as a cure."[13]

Being told to look on the bright side when you're suffering can be frustrating

JUST BE
RESILIENT!

COVID

YEARS IN
QUARANTINE

HATE CRIMES

UNCERTAINTY

when coming from a friend, family member, or acquaintance, but it's particularly galling when institutions and society at large use resilience as a way to sidestep responsibility for protecting people's mental well-being. In 2020, amid concerns about the economy, their families, and their health, people became twice as likely as in previous years to feel overwhelmed by changes at work.[14] The same year, nearly 75 percent of employees reported experiencing burnout at least once.[15] And while burnout was almost universal, it was particularly bad for working mothers: nearly three million women dropped out of the labor force during the pandemic.[16] As a source told psychiatrist Pooja Lakshmin, a women's mental health specialist, for an article about how her patients struggled during COVID, "The crushing toll on working mothers' mental health reflects a level of societal betrayal."[17]

So we're proponents of resilience, but not the kind that places blame on the individual or absolves leaders and institutions from their obligation to make structural improvements. There's a huge gap between demanding that everyone be mentally tough and helping them take care of their mental health. We'll spend the rest of this chapter walking you through a few mind-sets and strategies for how to better navigate uncertainty. Unfortunately, while the forces that cause uncertainty and anxiety are often not your fault, how you respond *is* your responsibility. But our goal is not to help you continue to battle for survival in a toxic environment. We want to help you achieve whatever outcome is best for you. That might mean reframing your thoughts to feel less anxious. Or it might mean walking away from an unhealthy situation entirely.

· · ·

LIZ: *Obviously, I didn't die in the ambulance. I spent a day in the hospital and was then discharged into uncertainty.*

After my panic attack on the L, I refused to take more mood-altering medication, even when my migraines started to come back. Over the next few months, everything revolved around pain. I would start scanning my body the moment I woke up. Was that a normal, minor muscle spasm, or the early rumblings of something more sinister? I went to work but then hurried back to the quiet, dark embrace of my apartment. I was too embarrassed to reply to concerned emails and texts. How could I explain what was going on? From the outside, I looked perfectly healthy.

I hit an emotional wall a few months later, on my birthday. By 3 P.M., I still hadn't gotten out of bed. My mom was now calling me every hour. Each time I picked up, she sounded more and more worried. I was worried, too. I'd never felt this low before. Was this going to be the rest of my life? Just a bleak mixture of work and hiding under the covers with the blinds closed?

Looking back, I think some kind of instinctual survival mechanism must have kicked in that day. I was suddenly absolutely beside myself. The force of my fury made me sit up in bed. This was unfair and unfun and I was f*cking over it. I wanted to hug my mom and put *on nail polish and go to a diner with friends and shove a greasy cheese-burger in my mouth. I wanted to claw back some control over my life.*

For the next five weeks, I religiously tracked my schedule, moods, and migraines to see how they might be related. I scoured WebMD and migraine message boards for nonmedication treatment options. Based on what I learned, I cut out alcohol and chocolate, avoided the sun like a vampire, and made sure to be in bed at 9 P.M. to get a full night's rest. I signed up for acupuncture on Tuesdays and Thursdays and started going to a nearby gym to get in thirty minutes of moderate exercise every day.

I decided to stick to my routine religiously for six months and see how it went. At that point, if my migraines were still bad, I'd recon-sider medication or look into other, more intensive treatment options.

That also meant turning down business school. I had been admit-ted to Stanford, but the lifestyle I'd need to follow to thrive there seemed completely at odds with what I needed to do to take care of myself.

I also put safeguards in place for when my anxiety threatened to take over. I made myself a "brain cotton candy" list, which included Twitter memes, the r/aww subreddit (photos of cute animals), and news about the Kardashians. In moments when I started to sink into rumination, I would force myself to take out my phone and ingest brain cotton candy. I started to see friends again, though usually for air-conditioned lunches instead of 8 P.M. dinners outside in the heat and humidity.

I'm far from "cured." I'll never be able to lie on a sunny beach for hours without paying for it later. I still have a flare-up once every few months. But I'm able to manage my atypical migraines and live my life, and I don't let worries about the future consume me anymore. I take care of myself, and then I take it day by day.

HOW TO WORK THROUGH IT

There's [an] art of being at home in the unknown," writes author Rebecca Solnit, "so that being in its midst isn't cause for panic or suffering."[18] People who learn to become more comfortable with uncertainty tend to rely on processes to help them navigate chaos. Those processes usually focus on two things: decreasing the amount of risk we expect and boosting our belief that we can handle uncertainty. This takes practice, but over time, you can feel more confident and start to see uncertainty as less overwhelming.

When we confront a wall of uncertainty and anxiety, there isn't a magical code word that will make it crumble away. Assume instead that the wall can be scaled by "a series of footholds of control," writes Stanford neuroscientist Robert Sapolsky, "each one small but still capable of giving support."[19] Here are some of those footholds.

1. Stop and sit with uncertainty

Navigating uncertainty starts by pushing back against our natural impulse to run from discomfort. Reader Alisa told us she used to do this—run from discomfort—all the time through what psychologists call *anxious fixing*. She'd feel a prickle of anxiety and instantly jump into action mode. She would set herself small goals—mail a letter, vacuum the living room, finally chime in on that group-text thread—and then rush to accomplish them. In the moment, it felt great to cross things off her to-do list. But it also meant Alisa wasn't actually working through the root cause of her anxiety. So even after a flurry of activity, she wouldn't feel any relief.

At its core, anxious fixing is about trying to regain a sense of control and progress. Sometimes that can take forms other than goal setting: at the start of the pandemic, Liz started consulting her horoscope for the first time in her life, while Mollie dove into history books that tried to explain how our society got to this level of uncertainty. None of these coping mechanisms were necessarily bad, but even the most harmless distraction can prevent you from focusing on what actually matters. Learning that there was going to be a new moon in Sagittarius distracted Liz for an hour, but it didn't help her feel more secure about her future.

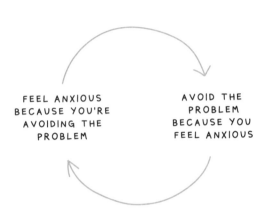

ANXIOUS FIXING

FEEL ANXIOUS BECAUSE YOU'RE AVOIDING THE PROBLEM

AVOID THE PROBLEM BECAUSE YOU FEEL ANXIOUS

Instead of making busyness a barrier to your anxiety, stop, acknowledge it, and sit with it. We even encourage you to honor it. After all, it's trying to protect you from something. "If you're too comfortable with uncertainty," psychology professor Kate Sweeny explains, "then you won't work to resolve it—and many more bad things could happen."[20]

Author Sarah Wilson likes to write a "No Bloody Wonder" letter to her anxiety. "I start, *Dear Anxiety, you funny little thing.* . . . I go on to acknowledge what it's up to, what it's feeling . . . and validate why it's got itself worked up. *No bloody wonder you're wobbly—you've been left in limbo for three days over a work outcome yet again. Plus you feel like you're in a rut, unable to get a clear view of why you're living.*"[21]

If your anxiety in the face of uncertainty is so intense that sitting with it sounds unbearable, remember this: strong emotions—those that cause a physical sensation in your body—last about ninety seconds.[22] We know that the urge to do something (anything!) when you're in peak panic mode can feel overpowering. The best advice we have is to force yourself to pause and just sit there. Tell yourself, "This will pass." Count to ninety. Or, if that sounds like too much, just count to five. Do it once and you'll likely find you can do it again.

Build the muscle of simply existing, and remind yourself that if you indulge in your urge, you'll just be perpetuating a cycle of feeling bad. You have to interrupt it to even begin to make change.

Other options for sitting with your discomfort include guided meditation (for our "List of favorite guided meditations," see pages 233–34), journaling,* therapy, and opening up to a friend. Or all of the above. None of these are quick fixes. But you can't skip learning to sit with yourself. You have to look your anxiety in the face and say, "Thanks for trying to protect me. I see you."

2. Adopt the mantra "I am a person who is learning _____"

Sitting with uncertainty forces you to confront the fact that you don't have all the answers. Especially if you're an overachiever who likes to feel in control, that can be frightening. You can't predict the future, which means you also can't perfectly plan for it.

But here's the thing: you don't need to have all the answers right now. Instead of beating yourself up for feeling anxious or for not knowing what will come next, reframe the situation. When we tell ourselves, "I am a person who is learning to _____," instead of "I can't do this" or "I need to have this all figured out already," we start to see ourselves as empowered agents of change.

In her most anxious moments, when the migraines were at their worst, Liz reminded herself, "I'm a person who is learning to cope with extreme uncertainty and stress. I'm figuring out how to prevent, or sometimes live with, a lot of physical pain."

Here are a few other examples of how you can reframe negative self-talk:

---

*Note: Research actually suggests that journaling is not always helpful, especially if you are stuck in an anxiety loop. Journaling can keep you too focused on analyzing whatever is causing your anxiety (which you may not have control over), leading to rumination. One way to prevent this is to journal as needed, rather than every day. For more information, we recommend Tasha Eurich's book *Insight*.

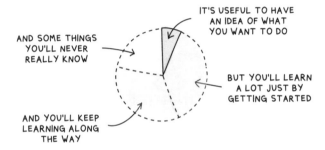

- "I feel so lonely; I shouldn't have moved" → "I'm learning to settle into a new city"
- "I'm such a bad parent" → "I'm learning to care for an infant and transition into a new life"
- "I don't know enough to manage people; I can't do this" → "I'm learning to be a great manager"
- "I'm a nervous wreck" → "I'm learning how to move through my emotions"

When we start to view ourselves as constantly learning and improving, we adopt what psychologists call a *growth mind-set*. A growth mind-set lets us see uncertain territory as an opportunity to learn something new. Uncertainty may still be challenging, but it won't be as threatening. A growth mind-set is the difference between hitting an obstacle and immediately thinking, "I don't know what to do right now, which means I can't do this," and telling ourselves, "I can develop the skills I need to overcome this."

(We want to add a caveat to this advice: You should never convince yourself that you are learning to handle a situation that is clearly harmful. If you feel as if you're being manipulated into something you don't want to do, as if your environment is leeching away your self-esteem, or as if you're in a situation that frequently makes you emotionally or physically sick, look for ways to get out.)

Small ways to ground yourself when everything is up in the air

When you're facing extreme uncertainty, it can be helpful to put routines in place—and to intentionally let some things go. Both serve as ways to establish enough stability to ease your anxiety.

Research shows that rituals or habits can go a long way toward reducing our stress levels. In fact, psychologists have found that it doesn't even matter what the rituals are. Simply doing the same thing at the same time can improve your mental health. Don't believe us? That's okay. Studies have also proven that rituals help people feel better even when they don't believe that rituals work![23]

Before COVID hit, Houston-based public school teacher Maxie Hollingsworth didn't wear much makeup, because she was always rushing from one place to another. But while quarantined, she found that wearing makeup was a way "to slow down and pay attention to herself."[24] Here are a few additional examples of soothing rituals that readers told us about:

- Commit to baking something delicious every Wednesday night
- Create a three-song playlist, and listen to it while dancing after work
- Dedicate an hour on Sunday afternoons to organizing a specific part of your home
- Do the seven-minute workout (you can find this on YouTube) each weekday
- Have the same breakfast every morning

On the flip side, we also recommend adjusting your expectations for yourself by intentionally letting some things go. At the start of COVID, writer and speaker Ijeoma Oluo recalled, "I got ready to shave my legs. And was like, 'Uh, I don't want to.' So then I didn't."[25] Before moving across the country, Liz's friend decided to start ordering takeout for dinner on Tuesdays and Thursdays and not worry about cooking. "I gave myself permission to put some parts of my life on autopilot," she told us.

The next time you're facing uncertainty, acknowledge that you're dealing with a lot. And then say, "I'm just not going to focus on ___ right now, and that's fine."

3. Translate your anxiety into specific fears

"I remember just sobbing into my orange chicken," our friend Caribay told us. "I kept thinking, 'I can't do this.'"

A few days before, Caribay had left Venezuela with her dad to fly to the United States and start her freshman year at Penn State. But as she stood in line to get her college ID, she started to panic. Her dad gently pulled her out of the line and walked her to a nearby Panda Express.

"You don't have to do this," Caribay's dad said when they were sitting down.

"You can come home with me this afternoon. I want you to know that whatever you choose, you will be fine." As Caribay calmed down, her dad asked if she wanted to get back in line, but the thought made it hard for her to breathe again.

Instead, Caribay and her dad decided to walk around the campus. "Let's look into some classrooms," her dad suggested, "so you can picture what it might be like to go here." They peeked into the library and then a large lecture hall. "That was also overwhelming to me at first," Caribay recalled. Up until that point, she had gone to a small school with the same twenty girls since third grade. "But seeing where I might sit every day did start to make me feel a bit better."

Slowly, Caribay's apprehension started to subside. "When I met my roommates," she told us, "they were really nice. I started to get a sense of 'Oh, I could see myself here. I could see myself doing this.'" A few days later, Caribay got back in line to get her college ID—and this time, she was filled with excitement.

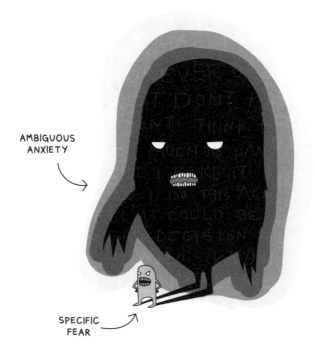

"We don't resist change," organizational psychologist Dr. Laura Gallaher told us. "We resist loss." By converting your ambient anxiety into more specific fears, you can pinpoint exactly what you're afraid of losing and how you might be able to avoid some of those circumstances. Often you'll find that you're scared of losing a part of your identity or of experiencing uncomfortable emotions in the future.

To gently surface the stories driving your sky-high heart rate, ask yourself:

- What am I afraid of?
- What do I imagine could happen?
- How exactly would each of those scenarios look and feel?

If you're starting a new role, you might write something like "The responsibilities I'm taking on are outside my past experience. I might not know what I'm doing, or I might look foolish. I'm most afraid that I'll fail and be fired." If you're moving to a different city, your answers might be "I'm worried I'll feel less at home. I'm scared I won't make new friends. In those scenarios, I'd be very lonely, and I might worry I made the wrong choice by moving. I'm terrified I'll regret my decision."

"I still get anxious when I have to make a big decision," Caribay told us. "But that campus walk taught me to think about what could happen in the future and visualize myself in all those scenarios." Years later, when Caribay was deciding where to go to grad school, she tried to paint a vivid picture of each option. One of the schools was in Chicago, but she couldn't afford to visit, so she ambled about the school's neighborhood using Google's Street View, scrolled through "Top 10 Things to Do in Chicago" listicles, and took a virtual tour of the campus. And when she was considering whether to take a job in San Francisco and had a bit more money, Caribay flew out to the city for a week. "I literally took the train to where I would work and grabbed a triple iced latte at a nearby coffee shop. I tried to give myself a very concrete idea of what that first day would look like."

While we were conducting interviews for this book, a lot of people told us that they find it useful to imagine the worst-case scenario. If that works for you, great. But if you are very prone to anxiety, be careful not to start catastrophizing. "Beware of that determined slide to the worst possible, barely imaginable scenario," Buddhist teacher Sharon Salzberg cautions.[26] It's useful to think through a high-probability worst-case scenario. It's less helpful to spend hours obsessing over a truly terrible outcome that most likely won't happen.

To make sure you're not creating even more anxiety for yourself, we encourage you to also ask:

* Is there evidence for my fear, or am I making assumptions?
* What is the probability that my worst case materializes?
* What's the *best*-case scenario?
* What's most likely to happen?

WHEN YOU FIND YOURSELF THINKING:

WHAT IF THIS DOESN'T WORK?

BE SURE TO ALSO ASK YOURSELF:

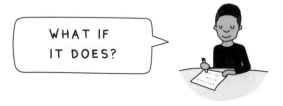

WHAT IF IT DOES?

Of course, sometimes a scary scenario isn't outside the realm of reality. Which brings us to the withins and the beyonds.

4. Separate the withins from the beyonds

"Grant me the serenity to accept the things I cannot change, the courage to change the things I can, and the wisdom to know the difference," goes a prayer attributed to the theologian Reinhold Niebuhr. Your fears will likely fall into two categories: those you can do something about, that are within your control (the withins), and those beyond your control (the beyonds). You have to be diligent about recognizing what you can't control. If you feel responsible for the beyonds, you'll never be able to say confidently that you've done enough.

Once you've listed your fears, go through each one and label it as a within or a beyond. Sometimes that's hard to determine. If you're not sure, try getting more specific. For example, you might expand "I'm afraid of getting sick" to "I'm afraid of getting sick because I've been taking on too many projects" or "I'm afraid of getting sick because I'm getting older." We would count the first as a within and the second as a beyond. That said, there's no objective line between them. Part of distinguishing between the two is picking what you can take on, and the rest is being honest about what is too much for you to bear right now.

Categorizing your fears can help you chart a clear course of action. "I experienced crippling anxiety over the state of the world in 2020," reader Susan shared with us. "I lived and worked in Manhattan during the height of the pandemic. The sounds of sirens were all I could hear. And reading the political news in America was anxiety-provoking." Susan's mental health took such a hit that her husband sat her down one evening to think through their options. They categorized the pandemic and politics as beyonds; those were out of their control. But they didn't have to stay in New York; where they lived was a within. "We decided to move to Toronto to get away and be close to my family—a choice I didn't think we'd be making."

Of course, you won't always be able to make such a big change. Reader Jayna also benefited from breaking her anxiety down into specific fears. "I hadn't dated at all after coming out of an abusive relationship four years ago," she told us. "Just the thought of it made me too anxious." Jayna decided to make a list of all her fears around dating. Based on what she wrote, she created a dating strategy for herself using the same approach she would use to develop a plan at work: knowing the audience (namely, herself), understanding common pain points (trust issues, falling for commitment-phobes), and developing solutions accordingly. While Jayna would never be able to know exactly how well a date would go or what the other person might do—those were beyonds—she did have control over where the date would be, how long it would last, and the uncomfortable questions she would ask to get to know the person better. "I put in place clear boundaries and values for my approach to dating," she told us. "It's working well so far—far from the chore it used to be. Now I've found myself having fun (!) and dedicating time only to the people who align with what I'm looking for."

5. The withins: Make a plan from which you'll deviate

In the face of uncertainty, you have to work extra hard to figure out what you should do next. We're hardwired to recognize patterns. When confronted with a known challenge (for example, driving a car or planning a trip), you can simply say, "Ah, okay, here is what worked last time. Let's do that again." Uncertainty breaks that mechanism. "You feel you have to pay closer attention to everything that's going on, because you're not confident about what you should do," psychologist Dr. Molly Sands told us.[27] "That's why uncertainty is so exhausting."

It's also why you might start thinking, *I'm so overwhelmed, I can't do this.* Your mind is swamped as it zigs and zags through a million future possibilities. Before Liz learned she was suffering from migraines, she would spend hours cycling through every possible cause of her headaches, from a brain tumor to her imagination. Focusing on your withins, and coming up with a plan for how you might handle each one, can give you a much-needed brain break.

The best way to approach the withins is to turn each one into an actionable question and then answer it. For example, take the fear "I'm afraid I'll get fired" and ask, "What would I do if I got fired?" Start to think of a couple next steps: you could post on LinkedIn that you're looking for a new role or reach out to friends to see if their organizations are hiring. "As an Indian immigrant in the United States on a visa," reader Madhura told us, "my long-term future in this country is uncertain." When she starts to worry about the future, Madhura asks herself, "What would I do if I had to leave the country? What are the resources I would need to secure a good future for my family, and am I working toward those? What would I lose and what would I gain? As I play this out in my head, it does not seem that daunting."[28]

Your plans and answers don't need to be highly detailed, so avoid getting swept up in analysis paralysis. The goal is just to build your confidence in the idea that you would be able to handle the situation. "When our brains are filled with unanswered questions," life coach Emily Nelson shared with us, "we feel unsettled and nervous. Your brain is trying to figure something out. Sit down, write out even a vague answer, and bring your power back in."[29]

You should not see your answers or plans as set in stone. The point of this exercise is mostly to reassure yourself that you're prepared to face what comes next. At NASA, Dr. Laura Gallaher told us, teams refer to agendas as "plans from which we deviate." As she explained, "The benefit of planning is doing the thinking around what we will do when something happens. The value is in the process and the journey, not in the specific agenda."[30]

Making a plan from which you'll deviate is informative and empowering and can help you feel calm even as you face an uncertain future. Most of all, you'll have realistic expectations; you won't feel guilty when things don't go perfectly, and you'll be more willing to see the journey as a learning experience.

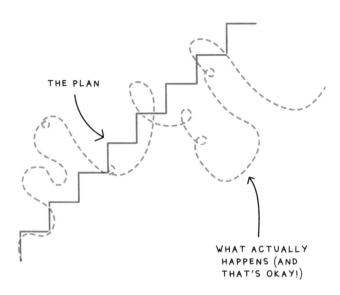

THE PLAN

WHAT ACTUALLY
HAPPENS (AND
THAT'S OKAY!)

It's also important to remember that the goal of this work isn't to be radiantly happy with the change but to acknowledge your authentic experience and set yourself up to take steps that feel good to you.

6. The beyonds: Let go of what you can't control

Yeah, we know. Easier said than done. For beyonds, a crucial piece of letting go is establishing boundaries around worrying—and sticking to them. During COVID, our friend Felix was scared for his father, who wasn't taking any safety precautions. "I realized there was only so much I could do," Felix shared with us. "I told my dad that I loved him, was worried about him, and hoped he would be more careful to avoid getting sick. And once I put that out there, I made myself move on. I guess I just forced myself to stop thinking about it."

So how do you just stop thinking about something, especially when it revolves around a frightening future? "Noting" can help. Noting simply means naming what you're feeling. The next time your mind starts racing with thoughts about a beyond, give your feelings a one-word label. *Resisting. Catastrophizing. Spinning.* By recognizing and naming your thought patterns, you can stop yourself from getting caught up in them so completely. "In that moment is the realization that we are not our thoughts," explains Andy Puddicombe, the founder of meditation app Headspace. "And that in itself can have a profound effect on the experience of stress and anxiety."[31]

You also can try this popular cognitive behavioral therapy technique: Dedicate a specific time to letting yourself worry about the beyonds. When you start to ruminate, tell yourself, "I'll come back to this tomorrow morning at nine." Scheduling a block of time when you'll give yourself explicit permission to cycle through your anxieties can help you more quickly set them aside in the present.

WHAT TO DO WHEN YOU FEEL ANXIOUS

TAKE DEEP
BREATHS

GO FOR A
BRISK WALK

MEDITATE
BRIEFLY

FOCUS ON A
PUZZLE

SUMMON A DARK
SPIRIT TO VANQUISH
YOUR ENEMIES

HUG A FURRY
FRIEND

7. Reflect on moments that bring you confidence

While you can't accurately predict the future, you can increase your confidence that you'll be able to get through whatever life throws at you.

Successfully navigating change is not about trusting the world; it's about trusting *yourself*. For forty years, researchers followed all the children born in Hawaii in 1955. The individuals who best coped with uncertainty tended to "meet the world on their own terms" and use "whatever skills they had effectively."[32] Most important, they believed that their actions could affect what happened.[33]

A powerful way to build confidence in yourself is to look back at everything you've already gotten through. Ask yourself:

- When have I felt unsure about my next steps?
- How did I get through that?
- What did I do well?
- What did I learn?

Remembering that you were able to cope before can help you see that you'll be able to do it again. Too often, our self-narrative in the face of uncertainty is "I can't do this. I'm weak and pathetic. I deserve to feel bad about myself" (actual train of thought from Liz). By reminding yourself that you've gotten through all your hardest days so far, you can more easily shift to thinking, "I'm not sure what will happen, but I'll be okay. I know I can handle it."

Sometimes it can also give you strength to think of what others have overcome. "When my parents came from Venezuela to Iowa to do their PhDs, they didn't know any English and had three kids under the age of ten," Caribay told us. "I have a vivid memory of my mom in our old kitchen, lining up a rice cooker, a slow cooker, a toaster, all these gadgets. She would press a button on each machine and then study and cook for us at the same time. She just made it work."

In Caribay's last semester of college, the political situation in Venezuela worsened so much that the government froze outgoing bank transfers. That meant that her parents, who had moved back after graduate school, were unable to send her money for her tuition. Caribay had a few days to come up with $18,000 or she wouldn't be able to graduate. And she made it work. She borrowed money from her friends and from a professor whose

PERCENTAGE OF YOUR WORST DAYS YOU'VE MADE IT THROUGH

100 %

lab she was managing. "It was so stressful," she recalled. "But now, when I think of my parents and I look back at that experience of really having to ask myself, 'Are you too proud to ask for help?,' I just know that no matter what happens, I will be able to figure it out."

You can also start taking small, consistent steps outside your comfort zone. In the midst of a breakup and a particularly difficult semester of school, reader Daniela's anxiety hit an all-time high. "I set up a challenge for myself where I tried one new thing a day for a month," she told us. "The new things ranged from simple stuff, like trying a new coffee shop, to eating at a new restaurant, to starting to play a new sport." Bit by bit, Daniela learned to trust in her ability to handle novel and stressful situations.[34]

8. Design your life based on your tolerance for uncertainty

Reader Dylan initially wanted to make a life in comedy but started to struggle with his irregular schedule and unpredictable income stream. Though he had booked a few high-profile stand-up shows, he was frustrated that his success still depended on getting lucky or getting picked by someone else. After two years as a comedian, he's now happily on a more stable career path in medicine.

Especially in our twenties, we're often made to feel that uncertainty is fun and adventurous. We're here to say: it's 100 percent fine to be "boring" if that's what makes you feel best.

How much uncertainty we can handle varies from person to person (for our Uncertainty Tolerance Assessment, see page 226). And while you can never predict the future, some choices do tend to involve less risk than others. Professors and career government employees usually have more stable jobs than artists and entrepreneurs. Our desire for security can also change and tends to increase with age (although midlife crises can cause a dip). Allie, an entrepreneur, told us that starting her own business "seemed sexy in my twenties but not so much in my thirties. I used to say, 'I don't want to know what the rest of my life will be like; that's boring.' Now I wish things were more boring."

It's okay to admit to yourself that you want more stability in your life. If your current situation involves a great deal of uncertainty and is causing you chronic stress, you may want to chart a new, less question-filled path. Reader Sonja has a nomadic history: she moved ten times in eight years, including two international moves. But the constant pick-up-and-go started to wear on her. She has now been in the same apartment for over three years. "I can finally buy plants," she told us.

. . .

Uncertainty makes us anxious. And even if COVID had never happened, we all would go through profound periods of uncertainty that leave us spinning and scared about what comes next. But with the right tools, we can gain confidence in our ability to better handle whatever life throws at us—whether that means establishing rituals to cope or charting a completely new, less stressful course for ourselves. We hope that the steps previously outlined can help you start to look at uncertainty with a sense of curiosity, rather than see it as an overwhelming force that always leaves you Googling "How to fall asleep" at 3 A.M.

TAKEAWAYS

- You cannot perfectly predict or plan for the future
- Face your anxieties and articulate them as specific fears or stressors
- Distinguish between fears or stressors that are within your control and those that are beyond it
- For the withins, create a plan from which you'll deviate
- For the beyonds, try to let go by noting, or by distracting yourself
- To build your confidence, look back at situations where you've been resourceful
- Aim to build a lifestyle that complements your uncertainty tolerance

CHAPTER 2

Comparison

Never compare your inside with someone else's outside.

Hugh MacLeod

MOLLIE: *"I'm sorry that I haven't returned your calls or reached out to you in so long. But I'm not in a good place right now," I texted one of my best friends from high school, Vanessa.* "I hope you can understand."*

Normally, Vanessa and I talked on the phone every other week at least. After decades of friendship, we had the kind of seamless relationship where we knew all the ups and downs of each other's work and personal lives. Since college, Vanessa and I had been on the same track. She wrote a book, and then I wrote a book. She got married, and then I got married. Then Vanessa got pregnant and I didn't. I went to see her in the hospital after she gave birth.

In that moment, I had felt so happy for her and as if we were as connected as ever. But soon after, my life fell apart. I got injured, decided to move across the country, and was so stressed that my period went away entirely. All the while, Vanessa seemed to hit milestone after milestone. She was living the life that I'd expected I would live, too.

And while I wanted to be happy for her and celebrate her successes, talking to her started becoming too painful for me. Every call was a reminder of how far behind I was and how poorly, in my eyes, my life compared with hers. As it turned out, it wasn't so easy being friends when our lives were no longer in parallel.

---

*Name has been changed.

• • •

Have you ever been exhilarated about hitting a professional or personal milestone only to find yourself, less than twenty-four hours later, having an Instagram-triggered crisis and tumbling down a black hole of I'll-never-be-good-enoughs?

MY SELF-ESTEEM

SEEING WHAT SOMEONE ELSE HAS ACHIEVED

You're not alone. In one study, more than 75 percent of people reported that they had recently assessed their self-worth by comparing themselves with others.[1] The modern world makes it hard *not* to constantly track your progress against someone else's: Glassdoor salaries, home square footage, vacation selfies, and your Bumble date's high school soccer stats can be instantly summoned with a Google search.

Even if you don't seek out the details of someone else's life, you're bound to stumble upon them. Mollie once got a glimpse of a gift-wrapping station in her boss's home office while on a video call and immediately felt inadequate. "I'm not organized or crafty enough to have a gift-wrapping station," she agonized. "Am I ever going to be at that level?" What *that level* meant wasn't even clear to her: Did she want to be a CEO, be craftier, or just have a partner who would set up a gift-wrapping station?

We're guessing you've found yourself in similar spirals. Relentlessly pitting ourselves against others can make us resentful, anxious, and impulsive (true story: people are more likely to go bankrupt after their neighbor wins the lottery).[2] Comparison and envy also make us feel ashamed. "Envy is an ugly two-headed monster," says psychology professor Dr. Christine Harris. "One head wants what someone else has. The other head chews on the first for having these negative feelings."*[3]

So how do you curb the downsides of comparison? Counterintuitively, science shows that what makes us miserable isn't comparison itself; it's when we don't compare ourselves to others *enough*. That might sound ridiculous at first, especially if you believe the saying "Comparison is the thief of joy" (which has been attributed to President Theodore Roosevelt and others).

But comparison doesn't have to dredge up so much pain. Humans are a relational species, so it's natural to wonder how you measure up. And observing others can be a source of motivation: Watching swimmer Michael Phelps win one Olympic gold medal after another can inspire us to get in the pool. And hearing about how her friend had successfully negotiated a raise spurred Liz to do the same a few months later. It's only when we don't know how to decode our emotional responses that we flounder.

In this chapter, we'll prove that comparison is inevitable and that the key to a healthier, happier you is to embrace it—without letting it spiral out of control. We'll walk through frequent misunderstandings about comparison and show you the benefits of pulling out your measuring stick more often. Finally, we'll

---

*A note on definitions: We often use the words *envy* and *jealousy* interchangeably, but they actually mean slightly different things. Envy is the feeling of desiring or idolizing other people's achievements, advantages, or wealth—for example, if you see a friend advancing in her career and you wish you could, too. Jealousy is seeing what someone else has and wishing you had it instead, as when a coworker gets a promotion and you wish it was you who had gotten it. *Jealousy* can also be used to describe the feeling when you want to protect what you have from others—for example, if your significant other is flirting with someone else.

leave you with a list of straightforward tips for what to do when your inner green-eyed monster is about to grab the wheel and run you off a cliff.

MYTHS ABOUT COMPARISON

Myth #1: Get off social media and you'll be free from comparison

Social media is extremely fertile ground for comparison. We (Liz and Mollie) have certainly done our fair share of scrolling and self-loathing. And we've both set social media boundaries for ourselves: Liz has a Google Chrome plug-in that hides the news feed when she's on Facebook, and Mollie doesn't have Instagram on her phone.

But getting rid of social media won't magically make your comparison tendencies disappear. Unless you vow to live by yourself in the backwoods with no cell phone reception, you will always be able to find someone who is having a more fabulous time than you are—while looking effortlessly fashionable and sailing up the corporate ladder. As one study shows, it's mathematically proven that your friends are much more likely to have more friends than you do. (Look it up!)[4] And more than 10 percent of our daily thoughts involve comparison, whether we're on social media or not.[5]

Comparison is central to

figuring out who we are.[6] Our accomplishments, expectations, and mood are all affected by how we stack up against others. In psychologist Charles Cooley's 1902 work *Human Nature and the Social Order*, he found that our self-worth stems, in part, from "the looking-glass self," or how we think we appear to others.[7] People see if they're "good" at something—and then feel "good" about their abilities—by checking whether they're better at it than others or by receiving praise for their talents.

We're not the only species whose emotions are guided by comparison. Researchers at Emory University found that monkeys judged their food by peeking at what other monkeys were munching. When every monkey was served a slice of cucumber, the group happily chomped away. But when some monkeys were given a sweet, juicy grape (a major upgrade), those who were stuck with the cucumber slices basically went apeshit.[8]

It's also evolutionarily advantageous to be hard on ourselves. We all suffer from negativity bias, which makes negative experiences particularly emotionally significant. After Liz gave a presentation at work, her manager gave her a glowing review—and one tiny piece of critical feedback. Guess which comment Liz spent the rest of the day obsessing over? In theory, this tendency should motivate us to try harder and thereby ensure our continued survival. But in the modern world, we're programmed to beat ourselves up when we think we've failed to measure up.

As a graduate student, reader Anna deleted Facebook to avoid seeing posts highlighting her peers' publications, presentations, grants, and dissertation findings. "But all my insecurities would return during conference season as people talked about their work," she told us. "I often felt a bitter undercurrent of jealousy and inadequacy at conferences."[9]

To put it simply: Avoiding social media for a while can be useful (we'll talk about this more later in the chapter), but it doesn't mean your days of evaluating yourself against others are over.

Myth #2: When you finally ___, you'll stop comparing yourself with others and just be happy

I f it starts with 'I'll be happy when . . . ,'" life coach Tanya Geisler told us, "it's not a goal. It's a trap."[10]

Comparison mutates and evolves, so that even when you finally cross that long dreamed-of finish line, you'll likely soon start eyeing a new one. Reader Maggie told us that when she was twenty-six and single, she would sit across from her older sister and brother-in-law at family events and covet their happy marriage. But after Maggie met and married The One, her finish line morphed into kids. By that time, her sister had two boisterous minis, while Maggie and her husband were just talking timelines.

The nature of comparison is to continually reassess where we stand.[11] Researchers call the people against whom we measure ourselves *comparison targets*—and these shift over time and as our circumstances change. Mollie's comparison target was Vanessa, but after Vanessa had had children and Mollie hadn't, that slowly changed. This can also happen at work. Say you're finally promoted to manager; other managers will suddenly be your peers. What once seemed out of reach is now something that most of the people around you have accomplished. This is called the "new level, new devil" phenomenon: every time you level up, you'll be surrounded by a new, more accomplished group of people—and you'll start to compare yourself with them.

As a law student, reader Kristin dreamed of being selected for the Presidential Management Fellows Program, a prestigious government program offering paid fellowships with government agencies that accepts only 3 percent of applicants. Her law school told her that they hadn't seen anyone reach the final interview round for over five years. But Kristin was determined. She went through twenty interviews in four weeks while balancing school, her part-time job, and her post as editor in chief of an academic journal.

One night, while out at a hotel bar with friends, Kristin got a phone call. It was the program coordinator, offering her a fellowship. "I sat in the lobby and cried with relief," she told us. To celebrate, she went to lunch with friends the next day, got fancy drunk on martinis, and then treated herself to a massage.

But Kristin's initial euphoria soon wore off, and she started to envy corporate lawyer friends who, as she describes, "were going to Greece for a month on their signing bonus, which was over 50 percent of my starting salary. Even though I was signing up for a career that meant a lot to me personally and professionally, I suddenly felt like a shadow. I felt like I wasn't going anywhere."[12]

Myth #3: The less you compare yourself with others, the better

When Priscilla became the first person in her family to graduate from college, part of her felt like a failure.

From the outside, Priscilla's life read like a success story about the power of perseverance. She worked two part-time jobs to pay for school, lived at home so she didn't need to worry about rent, and attended a community college for most of her credits. After receiving four associate degrees and a business certificate, Priscilla secured enough grants to cover the cost of enrolling at her local state university. There, she finished her bachelor's degree in just one year.

But all Priscilla could focus on was the fact that her journey to graduation had taken seven long years. Almost everyone else she knew had done it in four. A few years earlier, Priscilla had scrolled through an endless photo stream of her high school classmates cheering in their caps and gowns, and she'd plunged into despair. "I almost gave up a few times and almost dropped out," she recalled.

The night of her graduation, Priscilla lay in bed and tapped through filters on a couple of the photos her parents had taken. But she couldn't bring herself to post them to her Instagram. "How can I be excited to finish this when everyone did it already in half the time?" she thought to herself. She closed the app and pulled the covers over her head.

Too often, we draw comparisons that torpedo our self-esteem. But chances are, when comparison sends you down a dark spiral, it's because you're not comparing yourself *enough*. You watch a ridiculously talented pianist breeze through Rachmaninoff's Piano Concerto No. 3, tell yourself, "I'm so bad at piano," and stop there. You don't think about the fact that that pianist spends every day practicing for hours and has been playing since he was a preschooler. Or you focus only on how long it took you to get a bachelor's degree, without giving yourself credit for what you achieved.

Research shows that we tend to compare our weaknesses with other people's strengths. When you compare more comprehensively, things start to feel more attainable. Priscilla needed to compare herself more to understand that she had overcome many more financial hardships than her peers had had to face. When she started to read statistics about how few people with parents who haven't gone to college earn a bachelor's degree, she began to feel proud of herself. "That helped me realize that it didn't matter how long it took me. I did it." A family friend also reminded her that life has one deadline: when you die. Every other marker or timeline is something you set up for yourself. Realizing she *had* accomplished her goal helped Priscilla start to overcome her self-doubt.[13]

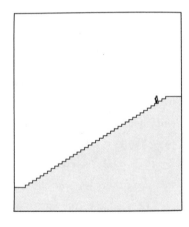

We'll talk more about this later in the chapter, but learning more about what others are going through can also help. When writer Aminatou Sow was battling cancer, a friend opened up to her about their financial problems. *"In my hour of cancer, other people are having problems too?? Please tell me everything!"* Sow wrote on her blog, recalling how it had brought her comfort to realize that she wasn't the only person in the world going through a hard time.[14] "It's possible your friends don't want to burden you with their own troubles," she explained. "It's thoughtful but it's also possible that it's making you feel like everyone but you is thriving."

• • •

MOLLIE: *My comparison targets were not limited to one perfect friend named Vanessa. Every time I went on Instagram and saw that another person was pregnant or had an adorable child, it felt like a literal punch in the gut. I could be having an okay morning, get bored and open Instagram, and then the rest of my day would be ruined. I found myself struggling to be the kind of generous and caring friend that I wanted to be. When my friends first started having babies, I sent each of them a hat that my mom knitted by hand. But as time went on, I stopped telling my mom about the newborns. I had to force myself to even respond to the baby-announcement emails or attend showers. I saw myself as a disappointing wife and daughter because we didn't have a baby. I still wanted to (and currently want to) have children, but I knew I needed to focus on healing from injuries first (see chapter 6, on despair). In my mind, my failure to have a child negated all my professional and personal successes. Here was this life milestone that everyone else was hitting and I wasn't.*

I realized that comparison was taking over my life and sapping my happiness and energy. The first step I took was to stop going on Instagram, cold turkey. That allowed the circle of people to whom I compared myself to get a lot smaller. It shrank enough that comparison was less likely to intrude and ruin my day. I still got texts and emails from close friends, but I didn't have to know that my college roommate's exboyfriend had just had twins and become a Bitcoin millionaire.

Every few months, I would go back on Instagram to look something up, and I was amazed at how long the images stayed in my brain. One ten-minute scroll would trigger feelings of comparison and inadequacy for weeks. The details of the lives of people I hadn't seen in decades would enter my dreams.

I also tried to spend more time around people who had taken a different life path. At our community pool, I made friends with a sixty-five-year-old woman and a ninety-nine-year-old woman, neither of whom had ever married or had kids. They both were content with their lives and didn't trigger any comparison for me. I reconnected with a friend from college who had gotten divorced at a young age. I put energy into friendships with people who similarly felt off-track.

It took a long time of purposely avoiding the types of comparison I used to engage in and, at the same time, doing work in therapy to be able to accept myself with my current life circumstances. After more than a year, I found that I could start to reengage with a broader circle of friends and even occasionally go on social media without spiraling.

I reached back out to Vanessa and was able to be honest with her about how hard it had been to fall out of lockstep with her. I told her that I hadn't been talking to many people on the phone, but that it was especially difficult to talk to her because she reminded me of what I thought my life was supposed to be. I was scared to have that conversation. I put off that phone call for months. When I did talk to her, she gave me the gift of not guilting me for pushing her away. And we have been able to slowly rebuild our friendship and find ways to connect, even though we are still in very different stages of our lives. I am grateful for that.

HOW TO WORK THROUGH IT

J ust found out one of the girls my boyfriend dated before me is pretty," tweeted comedian Abby Govindan. "I'm sick to my stomach."[15]

Left unchecked, comparison can make you miserable. Seeing people be better at something than you are can feel like a vicious uprooting. But with the right

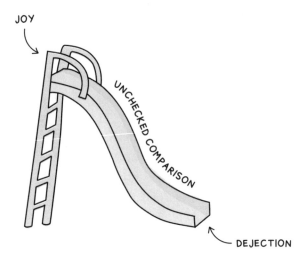

tools, you can use your envy to uncover what you value. In this section, we'll help you figure out how to decode what envy is trying to tell you and then turn your emotion into action. We'll also show you the blind spots that might be skewing your perspective on where you are relative to others.

1. Listen to your strongest triggers

Twenty years ago, while waiting for coffee to brew, a young lawyer absentmindedly flipped through her law school's alumni magazine. She breezed past an op-ed on the state of the electoral college, a long list of wedding announcements, photos of a fiftieth reunion. She landed on a section in which alumni shared career updates. Unsurprisingly, many had continued to practice law. Reading about some of their prestigious achievements, she felt a slight pang of jealousy.

But when she read about an alum who had become a full-time writer, her stomach dropped like an elevator. She had long entertained the thought of becoming a journalist or writing a book, but given how much she'd invested in her law career, she'd always relegated that idea to the land of daydreams. Now, reading about someone who *had* taken the leap, she was overcome by envy so powerful it left her on the verge of tears.

This is how *New York Times* bestselling author Gretchen Rubin decided to pursue a career as an author. Her career change didn't happen because of a conversation with her boss or months of visits with a life coach. It happened because she felt desperately envious of someone else's life.

Comparison can teach you what you value: you're more likely to feel intense admiration when you see someone doing something that you want for yourself—even if you haven't consciously allowed yourself to want it.

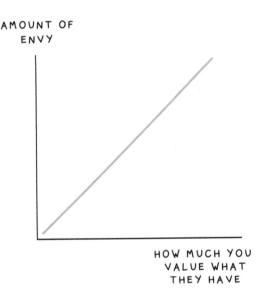

AMOUNT OF
ENVY

HOW MUCH YOU
VALUE WHAT
THEY HAVE

Self-awareness helps you turn your feelings into something useful. The next time envy rears its head, explore what it's telling you. Ask yourself:

- What do they have that makes me feel less than?
- What void do I believe having it would fill?
- Do I really want what they have?
- If yes, how much, and is it worth taking action to try to get it for myself?

The more specific your answers, the better you'll be able to redirect your emotion into actions and strategies. Reader Helen told us that she felt a wave of envy when she ran into a recently divorced friend in the grocery store. "She was glowing," Helen recalled. "At the time, I was really miserable in my marriage. Seeing her so relaxed and happy ruined my whole day." Helen didn't want a divorce, but she did want to rebuild her connection with her husband. A few weeks later, the couple started going to therapy together.

It can also be helpful to notice what you do *not* envy. One of Liz's close friends knew from an early age that she didn't want kids. "When I see photos of someone with their baby, I don't feel an ounce of jealousy," she told Liz. "It just makes me even more certain that while I'm happy for my friends with children, it's definitely not for me."

2. Make sure your envy doesn't become malicious

Comparison-induced envy can be a great motivator and guide. It can also make us bitter.

Psychologists distinguish between *benign envy*, when we admire someone and try to emulate them, and *malicious envy*, when we dislike and begrudge the other person for having what we want. It's the difference between "They have a penthouse apartment, and it's cool how they got it" and "I hate that their home has panoramic views, and I want them to suffer." To be clear: both are painful. But benign envy motivates us to work harder to improve, while malicious envy makes us nasty.[16]

We often feel malicious envy when we perceive scarcity. But in many cases, another person's ability to achieve something is evidence that it's possible for us, too. A group of researchers studied over six hundred lymphoma and breast cancer patients to uncover the effects of their interactions with one another. To their surprise, they found that group activities led to significant increases in self-esteem among the cancer patients who were the worst off.

IT APPEARS YOU'RE
EXPERIENCING
MALICIOUS ENVY...

Instead of feeling envious toward those who were doing well, these patients used the others to inspire hope and motivation.[17]

To shift your thinking from malicious to benign envy, try these phrases we heard from reader Aya:

- "I'm inspired by _____. Maybe I can learn from them, or ask them to be my mentor."
- "I haven't done what they've done . . . yet."
- "Every person is on their own journey. I'm grateful for mine."
- "If my favorite role models stopped what they were doing, I wouldn't be able to enjoy their incredible work."

That said, sometimes your malicious envy will seem warranted. Reader Ali seethed with jealousy when a better-connected but less competent colleague got promoted and she didn't. And our friend Paul, who grew up watching his mom struggle to make ends meet, told us that he often feels resentment toward a coworker who was born with a trust fund. Life is not fair, and unfortunately, you will have that fact shoved in your face over and over again.

When you feel yourself sinking into the stew, ask yourself: Is this person worth so much of my energy? To reclaim your attention and focus, figure out what other emotions you're experiencing and what you can do to move forward. Ali also felt angry, which motivated her to apply for better jobs elsewhere. And Paul combats the insecurity he sometimes feels by telling himself, "This line of thinking is really not productive for me."

3. Piece together the footage that was cut from someone's highlight reel

In 2010, Johannes Haushofer, today an associate professor of economics at Stockholm University, composed his "CV of Failures" to help students realize that rejection is part of the path to success. An updated version, posted on his university web page, includes sections like "Degree programs I did not get into" and "Academic positions and fellowships I did not get." He explains: "Most of what I try fails, but these failures are often invisible, while the successes are visible. I have noticed that this sometimes gives others the impression that most things work out for me. As a result, they are more likely to attribute their own failures to themselves, rather than the fact that . . . applications are crapshoots, and selection committees and referees have bad days."[18]

Most of us believe that other people live richer lives than they actually do.[19] And for good reason: in a recent survey, 82 percent of respondents admitted to making their lives look more glamorous than the reality, either by omitting the boring parts or by making it seem as if they're more out-and-about than they are IRL (in real life).[20] Psychologist Mai-Ly Nguyen Steers calls this seeing "everyone else's highlight reel."[21]

But we usually don't know what's really going on in someone else's life. And when we don't think through another person's behind-the-scenes, we're much more likely to feel malicious envy.[22] "Many people you believe to be rich are not rich," writes the author Cheryl Strayed. "Many people who seem to be gliding right along have suffered and are suffering."[23]

Early in her public relations career, Maria Ramirez's Facebook page looked fabulous. She posted photos of herself with the musician Juanes, backstage at Madison Square Garden concerts, and sipping cocktails poolside in Miami.[24] But offline, she was exhausted. She worked events until 2 A.M., was constantly on the road, and spent barely any time with her fiancé. It got "really old, really fast," she told *Fortune.* These

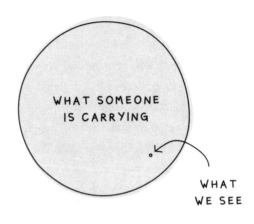

days, she has a less glitzy position but is much happier.

The next time you're overcome with envy because of a post or casual comment or LinkedIn update, take a step back and ask yourself:

- How do I know that this other person isn't struggling in some way?
- What am I proud of that doesn't show up on social media?
- What would others be envious of if I did share about it?

One final thing: it's possible to get too caught up in your *own* highlight reel. If you're applying filters to every photo you share, or only talking about the kudos you got from your boss, you risk feeling bad for not actually living the carefree life you're portraying. To make sure you don't end up longing for your own fantasy, think a bit more carefully about what you're trying to portray with the public stories you tell about yourself, and why. It's fine to share exciting life updates, but you might balance it out, or tone down the language so it's not overly sunny.

4. Avoid comparison hotbeds when you're feeling blue

On bad days, you're more likely to marinate in envy.[25] If your inner voice is already a livestream of negativity, it will twist any indication that someone else is better off into proof that you're destined to misery. Reader Susan told us that when she's down, she fixates on her friends' accomplishments to the point of feeling discouraged and deficient. "I'll visit people's LinkedIn profiles and obsess over how much everyone else has achieved."

In your more miserable moments, we recommend avoiding anything that is especially likely to trigger something called *upward comparison*, when you obsessively compare yourself with people you deem to be "above" you in some way. "When I go on Instagram, it's like socializing every second with everyone who's designed to make me feel the worst about myself," shared actress Cazzie David in an interview.[26] "My exes' new girlfriends, people who have the career I want, Kylie Jenner."

Of course, the times when you just want to lie in bed and wallow are also when it's easiest to pick up your phone and start mindlessly scrolling. Facebook data show that people spend 225 percent more time on the platform after a breakup.[27] This behavior can compound feelings of loneliness: researchers at the University of Houston found that feeling bad and then going on social media tends to give you a distorted perspective of your friends' lives, making you feel even more alone in your internal struggles.[28]

It can be helpful to set better boundaries for yourself. Make a list of people, platforms, or places that trigger upward comparison, and then have a plan for how you can avoid them when you're feeling down. We heard from many readers that they set a fixed amount of time (e.g., fifteen minutes a day) for checking social media. You can also set screen-time limits for specific apps in your phone's settings.

5. Pick a broader baseline

If you see a friend hitting a personal milestone, it's easy to feel you're far behind in life. But if you think of ten or twenty friends or acquaintances, chances are a bunch will be in the same boat as you—and might even be happily sailing along.

When Liz started drawing in her early twenties, she didn't measure herself against other beginners. She compared her work with pieces made by career art-

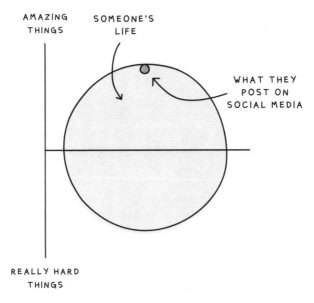

ists, who had gone to art school and perfected their craft for years. We all fall into this trap now and then. In an experiment, researchers asked people to assess their running abilities. They found that participants spontaneously compared themselves with *the best runner they could think of*, and deemed themselves not so great.

The researchers then prompted the participants to list the top ten runners they knew personally. By reflecting on the seventh- or ninth-best runner they had rubbed shoulders with, people suddenly felt a lot better. Comparing themselves with a broader group diminished the enormous gulf between themselves and what they thought of as "good."[29]

Psychologists also find that broadening your perspective can be helpful when you experience what they call *deprivation intolerance*: when you don't get what you want and that causes you to plunge into a pit of despair.[30] The next time you desperately covet what someone else has, swap out the question "Why don't I have that?" with "Do I have enough?" Chances are, you can survive without whatever it is you pine for, and not having it has no impact on your worth as a person.[31]

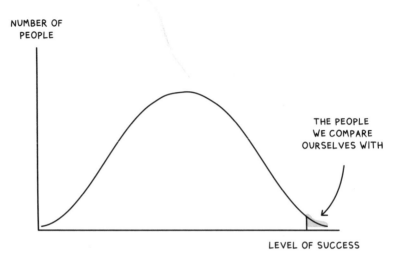

NUMBER OF
PEOPLE

THE PEOPLE
WE COMPARE
OURSELVES WITH

LEVEL OF SUCCESS

6. Compare the nitty-gritty

It's easy to wish you were making a million dollars a year from the corner office and ignore the responsibilities, stress, and long hours that come with the job. But you need to compare specifics.

A few years ago, Liz learned that a friend-of-a-friend had been promoted and would soon be leading a team of two hundred people. Liz was overcome with envy. That night, she lay awake questioning all her career choices. Liz has always found back-to-back meetings exhausting, and she generally prefers "doing the thing" to "managing the people doing the thing." She's never aspired to run a team of hundreds of people.

But there she was, sleepless and miserable about not managing. "Does my jealousy mean I should shift all my plans?" she wondered. "This whole time, have I been wrong about who I am and what I want?"

The next morning, Liz awoke with the certainty that she was still the same meeting-avoidant person—and that she didn't want to trade places with her newly promoted acquaintance. She wasn't actually longing for the day-to-day that came with being a manager of managers; she just wanted the prestige and social validation of being able to announce a big, exciting accomplishment.

Thinking through a day-in-the-life helped Liz realize that she didn't need to shift her entire career but instead should keep going in her current path and look for more opportunities to become more visible. It's useful to understand that you may not actually want your friend's big house but instead covet the prestige it communicates or the financial security it symbolizes.

Kristin, the lawyer who was envious of her corporate lawyer friends' incomes, also learned to better compare the specifics of her life and others'. When she thought about how meaningful she found her day-to-day and the fact that she didn't have to sacrifice her social life to work seventy-plus-hour weeks, she realized that her dreams had been well placed; she loved her career in public service.

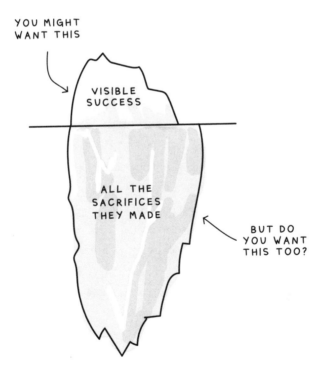

YOU MIGHT WANT THIS

VISIBLE SUCCESS

ALL THE SACRIFICES THEY MADE

BUT DO YOU WANT THIS TOO?

You should also consider the experience level and efforts of your comparison targets. When reader Aya was job hunting during her last year of college, she would often hear about someone landing an amazing position and feel crummy. One afternoon, a friend excitedly told Aya she had gotten a job at NASA. Aya felt jealousy rearing its ugly head, until her friend continued, "After applying for ninety roles, I can finally relax." It dawned on Aya that she had applied for only a few jobs so far. "We see people's achievements easily," Aya told us, "but the work it took to get there is often invisible."[32]

To sum up, here's a list of questions to help you make better comparisons:

- What would a day-in-the-life look like?
- What specific pieces of that life do I want?
- What specific pieces of that life do I not want?
- What experience does this person have?
- Is this comparison based on some imagined/better version of myself or other people's/society's expectation of me?
- Am I willing to give up the good things in my current life to have that?

7. Compare present you against past you

You may not always be exactly where you want to be, but chances are you're not where you *used* to be, either. Pausing to take stock of your accomplishments—and the skills you've developed as a result—can help you feel proud of your progress and untangle yourself from malicious envy.[33]

Though reader Eliza has always loved mountains, she avoided running or hiking for most of her life because her asthma left her at a disadvantage compared with her peers. In her late twenties, she finally decided to go for it—even if that meant going for it at a slower pace than most. "I will never be able to hike as fast as others," she told us. "I'll always be slower because of my low lung capacity. The only person I can and should compare myself to is me." Eliza's persistence and new attitude paid off: just before her thirtieth birthday, she completed a five-day hike.[34]

A simple way to make this type of self-comparison a habit is to take a few minutes at the end of each month to reflect on these prompts:

- What have I learned over the past few weeks?
- What was difficult, and how would I approach it differently given what I know now?
- What progress did I make?

Keep in mind that an important part of the progress you've made is what you learned. You might be starting over in a new place or have switched careers

WHAT IT CAN FEEL LIKE

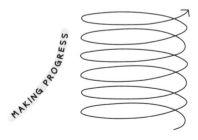

WHAT'S ACTUALLY HAPPENING

or left a relationship. That doesn't mean you're "behind" where you used to be. It means you're starting again, this time with experience.

. . .

Comparing yourself with others is unavoidable, but by applying some of the advice listed above, we hope you can learn to use it to your advantage. A good rule of thumb is to balance comparing up (looking at people who have more than you) with comparing down (looking at those who are worse off than you). And finally, remember that you only see the tip of the iceberg. Someone whose life seems perfect on Instagram may be dealing with struggles that you're completely unaware of.

TAKEAWAYS

- Deleting Instagram won't cure your comparison woes
- Use envy to pinpoint exactly what you value . . .
- . . . and then make a plan for how to move on
- Avoid comparison hotbeds when you're glum
- Remember: you're usually only seeing someone else's highlight reel
- Pick a broader baseline, and compare the nitty-gritty
- Look back at how far you've come, and celebrate your progress

CHAPTER 3

Anger

Anger is an assertion of rights and worth. . . .
In anger, whether you like it or not, there is truth.

Soraya Chemaly

LIZ: *As a child, I rarely saw my dad in the kitchen. While he was always supportive of me as an individual, he held traditional beliefs about gender roles. "Men don't cook or clean," he would tell me. "That's a woman's job. Women are made to have kids and take care of their families. One day, you'll want a husband and a baby over anything else. It's just what happens."*

I was defiant. My sole purpose in life was to cater to a man and be surrounded by screaming toddlers? I didn't think so. I would never be a "Mrs. Someone Else," and I had no plans to throw myself away for a husband or a baby. "Watch me," I seethed.

Decades later, when I was twenty-eight, I met Maxim. On our first date, he tossed together a green salad and stirred pesto into the pasta he had cooked. After dinner, he swept while I rinsed the dishes. I liked him.

We dated for four years before Maxim got down on one knee and popped the question. I was surprised by how many warm fuzzies I felt. I was going to get married, but I didn't feel like I was losing pieces of myself in the process. I was happy.

And then came the comments.

"Congrats on convincing him to lock it down!"

"That's amazing! You're so lucky! Mrs. Massenkoff has a nice ring to it."

"Since you'll be having kids soon, I recommend a C-section. All my friends who had vaginal births basically don't have a vagina anymore." (This was from someone I barely knew.)

At first, I tried to tell myself that people were just excited and well-intentioned. But it soon became clear that no such things were being said to Maxim. People told him, "Congratulations," and moved on. No "You're so lucky." No unsolicited parenting advice.

Every time Maxim was spared the wedding and baby talk, I felt a twinge of resentment, made worse by the fact that even when I tried to explain that I had no plans to change my name or immediately make motherhood my top priority, my protests were waved away.

"My wife kept her name until we had kids. Then she saw it makes more sense to be a family unit. You'll come around."

"Yes, definitely enjoy the honeymoon period. You won't have any time for yourself after you have children! When are you going to start trying?"

My blood started to boil. Had my dad been right? Was this the end of "Liz"? Suddenly people seemed to address me as a soon-to-be wife and mother and little else. It was also implicit that I should be elated by the abrupt dissolution of every other part of my identity. Anything less would make me a bad fiancée and a bad woman.

"You must be relieved to finally be getting married!"

"Are you going to start shredding for the wedding?"

I had no idea. All I knew was that I was hopping mad. At the comments, at the fact that I had agreed to get married, and even (a little bit) at Maxim.

● ○ ●

I n 1977, psychology professor James Averill was frustrated. When it came to anger, he thought other academics had it all mixed up. Researchers at the conferences he attended kept referring to anger as a base instinct that served no purpose and should always be suppressed. But why would anger be such a commonly felt emotion if it wasn't important in some way?

To test his hunch, Averill decided to survey the residents in a nearby town. The questionnaire he developed was fourteen pages long and asked people to "recall the number of times you became annoyed and/or angry during the past week" and to answer prompts like "In becoming angry, did you wish to get back at, or gain revenge?" Averill knew that answering so many questions was a lot to ask of someone and assumed that most people would just throw the survey in the trash.

He was wrong.

"It was the best-performing survey I've ever conducted," he told *The Atlantic* decades later. "Some people even attached thank-you notes. They were so pleased to talk about being angry."[1]

Averill's survey produced two important findings. First, most people said they felt mildly to moderately angry several times a week (and often, several times a day). Second, Averill discovered that, contrary to what his colleagues claimed, when people got mad, they were more likely to try to improve a bad situation.

ANGER

In the years since Averill's survey, a broad range of research has confirmed what his results revealed: anger can serve you if you channel it productively. "Anger is pain's bodyguard," says grief and loss expert David Kessler.[2] Getting mad can spark creativity, motivate you to advocate for yourself, and help you perform better in competitive circumstances.

PAIN

Of course, fury and frustration can eat you alive if you let them. In this chapter, we'll bust four harmful myths about anger and then offer you a set of strategies for how to better identify and meet the unaddressed needs behind your outrage. We'll offer strategies for how to communicate your feelings effectively and show you that sometimes anger is the key with which you can set yourself free.

MYTHS ABOUT ANGER

Myth #1: You should suppress your anger

When we were children, our parents and other adults often told us to *stop being angry!* And though gender norms are changing, girls tend to hear this more often than boys. Rage is usually presented as a particularly ugly and unfeminine emotion.

We also learn early on that the word *anger* can be associated with irrational violence, which makes us believe that when we're fired up, we're at our worst. "My grandma said that when you're angry, you hurt people," reader Karla told us about her childhood in the Philippines. "I am not so sure whether she meant that being angry can lead to physically hurting that person or hurting their feelings. But I believed both." For most of her life, when she got mad, Karla tried to suppress her rage. It rarely worked. Inevitably, she would explode, and in the process "utter words I never imagined I would actually say. I used to hate myself whenever I got angry."[3]

Karla's binary approach is more common than we like to believe, and it's one of the primary reasons we need to roll back the war on anger. That's because anger is evolution's way of telling us "Do something about this!" When you feel yourself getting angry, "that's automatic, you cannot control that," explains neuroscientist R. Douglas Fields. "Your unconscious mind has taken in enormous amounts of data and has determined that you are in a situation that is threatening and is preparing you to respond physically. . . . The only way this circuitry communicates to our awareness is through emotion."[4] Think of anger as a nonspecific alarm intended to move you out of harm's way.

In many situations, anger can even be a form of compassion. As philosophy professor Myisha Cherry writes, anger often "expresses compassion for the downtrodden and the desire for a better world. Anger at racial injustice makes people eager to do something about it."[5] In a famous 1981 speech, writer Audre Lorde also addressed "The Uses of Anger": "Every woman has a well-stocked arsenal of anger potentially useful against those oppressions, personal and institutional, which brought that anger into being. . . . Anger is loaded with information and energy."[6]

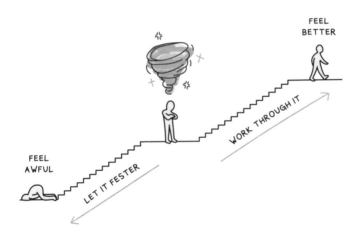

Plus, our attempts to suppress our anger usually don't work. Worse, when we pretend we can brush it aside, anger tends to fester into an even bigger and more difficult emotion, like resentment or hatred. The author Augusten Burroughs writes about this dangerous metamorphosis: "Resentment is anger looking for payback. It's also a high-interest-earning emotion. Each new resentment is added to the ones before. Long marriages have ended in ruin over tiny and insignificant grievances that were never properly aired and instead grew into a brittle barnacle of hatred. Hatred is clinical-strength anger."[7] In other words, the ire you feel when your partner loads the dishwasher "incorrectly" might be a signal worth unpacking.

Myth #2: We are reliable judges of who is angry

We may think that we are able to tell who is and isn't angry, but studies show that stereotypes and biases often cloud our judgment. Researchers have found that male faces, from infancy onward, are perceived to express more anger, even though participants believed that the male and female subjects *experienced* the same level of anger.[8] Yet surveys in 2015 and 2018 showed that women were more consistently angry than men.[9]

Racial stereotypes about anger can be even more pernicious. When tennis player Serena Williams had an argument with a referee at the US Open in 2018, he chose to call it verbal abuse and meted out the maximum penalty of a $17,000 fine.[10] SERENA ACTED LIKE A SORE LOSER, accused a headline in the *New York Post*.[11] In contrast, take Novak Djokovic, a white Serbian tennis player, who had an on-court outburst at the same tournament in 2020 after losing a serve. In a rage, he hit a ball in the direction of a line umpire and *struck her in the throat*. After he was disqualified, the *Post* ran a piece (by the same writer) titled NOVAK DJOKOVIC'S EXCESSIVE PUNISHMENT IS TERRIBLE FOR US OPEN.[12]

On a national level, school administrators mete out harsher punishments to Black students than they do to their white counterparts due to perceived aggression. Studies show that Black middle school and high school boys are much more likely to be seen as "troublemakers" than white boys, even if they exhibit the exact same behavior.[13] And Black girls are 5.5 times more likely to be suspended than white girls.[14] Pair that with research showing that Black women are less likely than a general-population sample to report feeling angry when faced with criticism or perceived disrespect, possibly to avoid the "angry Black woman" label.[15]

Asian Americans, on the other hand, are stereotyped as cold and competent rather than angry.[16] "The figure of the angry Asian American remains a void in the dominant American cultural imaginary," writes cultural and ethnic studies professor Dr. Nan Ma.[17] Phil Yu, a blogger who writes about issues affecting Asian

Americans, chose to call his blog *Angry Asian Man* to combat another pervasive stereotype: that Asians are quiet and passive. The "idea of the Angry Asian is very confrontational," he writes. "People don't really normally associate the two words together, and so when people see that, it's in-your-face provocative." But more than just provocation, Yu's blog title reflects an undeniable truth: "a lot of Asians are . . . very vocal, and they can get angry about issues affecting their community."[18]

There is a lot more than can be said here about this topic. We encourage you to check out our resources on anger on page 234.

Myth #3: Venting makes you feel better

Blowing off steam is not as productive as you might think, even though it's long been presented as a cathartic activity. In the 1980s, you could purchase a Wham-It punching bag toy for those explosive moments "when you feel like you just have to strike out." A clear vinyl pocket even let you insert a photo to pummel.[19] These days you can pay to go to "anger rooms" and smash TVs and dinner plates with a baseball bat.[20] It's also surprisingly common to hear about people who got so mad they punched a hole in a wall.

But research shows that this type of "destruction therapy" causes your anger to escalate rather than diminish.[21] Psychologist Brad J. Bushman studied people who used a punching bag to let out their anger, and found that "doing nothing at all was more effective" at diffusing rage.[22] Medical evidence also suggests that throwing a fury-fueled fit increases your risk of a heart attack by more than eight times.[23]

When you express your anger by lashing out, you run the risk of doing lasting damage—and of creating harmful habits. It's not helpful to leave a dent in your living room wall every time you're upset. Even just raising your voice can be scary or hurtful to others. And something said in a moment of rage is like toothpaste: you can never put it back in the tube.

Chronic venting, when you rehash the same problems without trying to understand or solve them, has also been shown to make you and the people listening to you feel worse.[24] "I finally had to put a limit on how much I trash-talked with coworkers," reader Paula told us. "I found that using the time to instead focus on how I could learn or improve made me feel a lot better."[25]

Myth #4: Anger is usually triggered by a specific event

Yes, a specific event can make you go ballistic. We heard from readers that they've lost their cool over all kinds of seemingly small triggers: inconsistent wi-fi, impossible-to-open packaging, too-frozen ice cream bending the spoon, an email from their boss that just read "?," their spouse asking when dinner would be ready.

But the sparks that make us explode usually have kindling. The "?" email came after months of condescending and curt interactions. A larger-scale example: when Brett Kavanaugh became a US Supreme Court justice, there was a public outcry (WOMEN REACT TO KAVANAUGH HEARING WITH RAGE AND PAIN, read a headline in *New York* magazine[26]), both because of his personal history and because he was emblematic of centuries of women being ignored after being sexually harassed or assaulted.

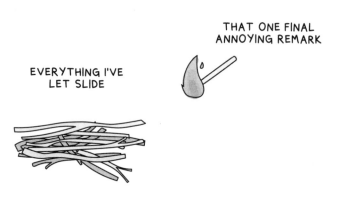

THAT ONE FINAL
ANNOYING REMARK

EVERYTHING I'VE
LET SLIDE

"Chronic stress literally rewires the rage circuits in your brain," writes R. Douglas Fields in *Why We Snap*.[27] If you're stuck in an unhealthy environment or under a lot of pressure, you develop an extremely short fuse. The sustained level of stress and fear you experience every day depletes your emotional resources, making you much more likely to get mad, even at minor provocations.[28] When you're miserable at work day in and day out, you become much more likely to snap at your spouse or a friend over Sunday brunch.

So, yes, one event can make you justifiably upset, but when examining your anger, try to more fully understand what might have already been cooking inside you. We will help you do that in the next section.

• • •

LIZ: *On a walk with my friend Carly, I ranted about the comments that getting engaged had unleashed. When I finally was done, she asked, "Has Maxim asked you to change your name?"*

"No," I admitted.

"Does he expect you to suddenly make it your sole purpose to cater to his every need?"

I considered for a moment and then shook my head. "No."

"Okay. And does he expect you to have kids right away, or quit your job when you do?"

"No, he loves hearing about my work."

Carly shook her head. "See? Getting married, or even having kids, doesn't mean you have to give up everything you care about. I know a couple whose policy is 'Me first, we second, kids third.' You and Maxim can just decide whatever you want."

On the drive home, I was struck by how much lighter I felt. Somewhere during the past few weeks, I had started to see Maxim and marriage as the enemy. But what was inside our relationship was good. I was angry about external forces, and terrified about what they might do to me and to us. Realizing that Maxim could be my partner in setting boundaries and building a life that felt fair was a relief.

Carly was right: Maxim had never pushed me—nor was he likely ever to do so—to become someone else, change my name, or give up my career if and when we had kids. Over and over, he had told and showed me that he loved me for everything that made me Liz, for everything that I valued about myself, too.

That night, Maxim and I sat side by side, opened a Google doc, and started to draft a list titled "Pieces of ourselves we love and don't want to lose (+ action items)."

We talked for a long time about what was triggering my anger. We started with the barrage of baby questions. In our Google doc, Maxim typed, "Liz doesn't want to have only wedding- and baby-focused conversations (if/when Liz is pregnant, Maxim will field all baby-related questions)." We moved on to my conviction that I wanted to keep working, both at my job and on my creative projects. We wrote:

- *Maxim and Liz both want to keep working (will figure out child care)*
- *We'll continue to prioritize frugality (Liz won't get sucked into buying a bunch of cute baby stuff that the baby will wear once)*
- *We'll give each other alone time when needed*

Finally, we touched on my anger at being asked if I was going to change my name. I wanted to stay Liz Fosslien as a symbol that I was still me, an individual, even though I was getting married. We added, "Liz won't change her name."

"Feel better?" Maxim asked me. I closed the computer and pulled him close. "I do," I replied.

UNHEALTHY CONFLICT
YOU
VS.
ME

HEALTHY CONFLICT
YOU + ME
VS.
THE PROBLEM

HOW TO WORK THROUGH IT

Anger finds a way

"Anger is like water. No matter how hard a person tries to dam, divert, or deny it, it will find a way," writes author Soraya Chemaly in *Rage Becomes Her*. When we internalize or suppress our anger for too long, it "threads itself through our appearances, bodies, eating habits, and relationships, fueling low self-esteem, anxiety, depression, self-harm, and actual physical illness."[29]

In this section, we'll help you better understand your anger triggers and tendencies and then outline strategies for how to more effectively identify and address the unmet needs behind your fury. Our aim is to empower you to respond, rather than react, to whatever is making you so $%^@#@ mad—and to avoid those chair-throwing, door-slamming moments you'll likely regret later on.

Respond Rather Than React

1. Identify your unique anger triggers

To better navigate anger, start by pinpointing exactly what it is that drives you up the wall. Your triggers might be events (perhaps you're unfairly passed over for a promotion) or conditions (for example, you haven't eaten in a while). If you're having a hard time coming up with a list, ask someone who lives with you or loves you—they will know. Liz's husband, for example, immediately answered, "When you feel like you're being misrepresented. And when someone chews gum next to you."

Our friend Candice often feels that her parents listen only to her older brothers, even though she usually takes a more reasonable stance and tends to fall into the role of organizing events and trips. "That's one of my biggest anger triggers," she told us. "When I think people are ignoring me or not taking my suggestions seriously, I snap." Simply acknowledging this trigger has helped Candice self-regulate in the moment. "I used to be really bad at sensing when I'm near my limit emotionally," she explained. "Now I notice what's happening much earlier, and I'm able to prevent myself from getting too worked up."[30]

Here are some common anger triggers:

- Feeling like you aren't being heard
- Feeling like decisions are made unfairly
- Being in a state of anxiety
- Being told to calm down
- When someone interrupts you midsentence
- When someone does something that affects you without your permission
- When you're about to do something and someone tells you to do it

Identifying your triggers can help you anticipate when your blood will start to boil, which makes it less likely that you'll experience what scientists call *amygdala hijack*, an emotional response that is immediate and overwhelming. When this happens, we're more likely to say or do things that we regret.

A few years ago, our friend Jake saw a driver in the next lane throw an entire bag of fast food wrappers out of his window. When Jake pulled up next to him at a red light, he rolled down his window and yelled, "F*ck you, stop littering!" The other driver looked outraged and started to get out of his car, but luckily the light turned green, and Jake was able to drive off. Recalling the story, Jake looked embarrassed. "I flipped out. And it almost got me into a road rage incident."

We recommend keeping an anger log, a journal in which you write down moments when you felt frustrated or irritated, for a week. This practice can help you identify patterns and then come up with a few ways to better move forward in the moment. Journaling helped reader Jesse figure out that he tends to be much more irritable when he's tired. Knowing that helps him realize that if he feels a flash of anger over something late at night, he doesn't need to act on it. He just needs to go to bed. (Side note: We hate the advice "Never go to bed angry." Go to bed angry! Sometimes you just need some sleep.)

2. Understand your anger expression tendency

In addition to your unique triggers, it can be helpful to understand how you tend to express anger. (You can find our Anger Expression Tendency assessment on page 221.) Here are a few of the most common anger expression tendencies.

Anger suppressor: You rush to tamp down your anger (this is often an unconscious process) and may have a tendency to blame yourself for the situation that caused you to be upset even when you are not at fault. In some cases, your anger makes you so uncomfortable that instead of freely feeling it, you feel a different emotion instead, like sadness or guilt. When anger is suppressed, it tends to lead to anxiety and depression. Anger suppression is also associated with hypertension and high blood pressure.

If you tend to suppress your anger, instead practice communicating it in ways that feel safe. Start with something small, like asking your partner to stop overfilling the dishwasher. When Liz was trying to become more assertive, she found this formula for communicating a particular anger issue helpful:

What the other person did +

the negative effect it had on you +

how it made you feel

For example, Liz would say, "You interrupted me during our presentation, so I didn't get a chance to finish sharing. That made me feel dismissed." While this strategy is simple, it's certainly not always easy to implement! We heard from many readers that they've found it helpful to set aside time with their partner, friends, or team specifically to work through frustrations. For example, one team hosted a retrospective meeting every Friday in which each person had a chance to share one thing that went well that week and one thing that could have gone better.

Anger projector: You frequently express your anger aggressively, toward either other people or objects. You may lash out physically (slamming doors) or verbally (insults, profanity, sarcasm).

Aim to lengthen the time between the anger trigger and your response, to give yourself a chance to cool down. We recommend a technique psychologists call TIPP, which stands for temperature, intense exercise, paced breathing, and progressive muscle relaxation. Because our brains translate our physiological reactions into emotion, you can calm your mind by consciously slowing your body's physiological reflex. Splashing cold water on your face, doing ten jumping jacks, taking deep breaths, and clenching and unclenching your muscles can all serve this purpose.[31] If you're unable to remove yourself physically from the situation, you can say something like "I'm having a strong reaction right now, and I need a moment." Reader Yalenka shared that to react less impulsively, she'll often state, "I'd like to come back to this later."

Anger controller: You do everything you can to appear calm, no matter how upset you are. You focus more on monitoring and controlling your expressions than on exploring what your anger is trying to tell you. You might be out of tune with your emotions and have a tendency to leave the situations that cause your anger unresolved.

Find ways to get more comfortable with your anger. That can be as simple as saying to yourself, "I'm upset, and that's okay." Work on naming and understanding your feelings, and let go of self-judgment. Try to uncover what's driving your emotions by filling in the phrase "Right now I feel ____ because ____."

Anger transformer: Your tendency is to resolve anger by recognizing it and understanding the deeper need. You use techniques like meditation, breath work, and patience to help work through anger in a productive way rather than suppressing it. You understand that anger can be clarifying and healthy (when not projected outward onto others or inward onto ourselves).

If you are an anger transformer, keep doing what you are doing. Notice when you slip into less healthy ways of expressing your anger and what the triggers are.

• • •

The way you express anger is often affected by how you were raised. Some people grew up in families who expressed anger through yelling, so they modeled their expression on that example. In some families, it's not safe to express anger, or it's acceptable for only one person to do so.

As a child of divorced parents, Mollie felt like she had to play the role of peacemaker and learned to suppress her own anger. But she knows how important it is to be able to express anger in a relationship, so she and her husband, Chris, check in every Sunday. They use the time to share what they think went well in the relationship during the past week, what could have been better, and what they have coming up in their individual lives. For two people who tend to avoid conflict or not express anger until it has boiled over, the weekly check-ins create a space where they feel safe giving each other feedback and can address small issues together before they become big.

Different cultures express anger in very different ways. As Erin Meyer writes in *The Culture Map*, people in Russia and Israel are generally more comfortable with confrontation, while individuals who grew up in Japan or Sweden tend to be more conflict-avoidant. We see variation even within different geographic regions of the United States. In New York City, it's not uncommon to hear people cursing each other out on the street, whereas in the South, you might hear someone say, "Don't rush on my account," when they actually think someone is moving too slowly.[32]

A final note: women tend to show up on the passive end of the anger-tendency spectrum. While boys are usually socialized to express their anger (either by talking about it or by dealing with it competitively), girls are often encouraged to understand the other person's perspective. As adults, that means women are far more likely to suppress their anger, sometimes without even realizing it. For women, tears are often a sign of anger, since women are not socialized to express anger by getting frustrated or yelling.[33] For men, depression can often manifest as anger, since they are socialized to avoid appearing sad.[34] Women may need to work harder to develop what Chemaly describes as "anger competence." She writes, "I wanted to own my anger, because it brought me back to myself. It gave me clarity and purpose."[35]

3. Acknowledge that a violation took place

Now that you understand a bit more about when and how you get mad, let's talk about what to do in the moment. First, give yourself permission to be angry. Because we receive so many messages that anger is bad, we often try to stamp out our feelings immediately, even in situations when we deserve to be infuriated.

While working abroad for a large multinational corporation, our friend Griffin was invited to go to lunch with his team. As the group stepped inside the elevator on leaving the office, a vice president suddenly reached his hand into Griffin's button-down shirt and began to caress his chest with his fingers. "Gay! Gay! Gay! Gay!" he chanted, egging the others on to join in.

Griffin spent the afternoon overcome by shame and confusion. "I grew up in a house where we weren't allowed to be angry or to complain, especially about a job or another person," he told us. "So I just went straight to anxiety and guilt."[36] He replayed the incident over and over, trying to figure out how he had brought it on himself. "I'm gay. I'm the outlier," he thought. "Maybe it's me who doesn't understand." But when he finally told a friend what had happened, she was horrified. "That's sexual harassment."

When a violation occurs, you are allowed to be unapologetically angry. Getting mad can give you a stronger sense of self—and the motivation to speak out. In March 2021, after a man in Atlanta shot and killed eight people, six of

whom were Asian women, a local law enforcement official claimed that his actions were the result of "a really bad day for him."[37] The comment caused outrage for two reasons. One, law enforcement was downplaying the actions of a white male killer. And two, the incident was an example of a broader, habitual diminishment of Asian American experiences. "Time and time again, Asian American experiences and voices have been diminished and ignored," explained writer Jennifer Li in a piece addressed to Asian American girls. "I need you to remember that you are not spoiled or undignified in having emotions. You are entitled to them. Anger is natural. Anger is healthy. Anger can be righteous."[38]

Simply recognizing that you're upset—and giving yourself explicit permission to feel that way—can be cathartic. "Just saying, 'I am angry!' to myself out loud or in my head helps me a lot," Karla told us. "When I admit it, I accept that part of me that I used to hate." And she finds that she's able to feel better faster than when she tried to squelch her anger.

4. Identify and address the need(s) behind your anger

To identify the specific needs behind your emotion, try writing an angry letter that you will never send. A few questions that might help you clarify the reason(s) your blood started boiling:

- What triggered my anger?
- What led up to this moment?
- What feelings are underneath my anger?
- What do I need to be okay right now?
- What longer-term outcome would make me feel better?
- What steps can I take toward that outcome?
- For each of those steps, what do I risk and what do I gain?

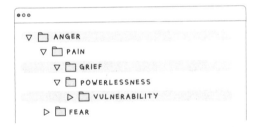

Anger needs to be addressed; otherwise, it becomes damaging. That said, we recommend giving yourself time to calm down before you make any major moves. When we're upset, we're less able to think strategically. If your heart is racing or your fists are clenched, pause for a few minutes. Liz has learned to evaluate her anger on a scale from 1 (irritated) to 10 (enraged) and aims to wait until she's settled down to a 3 or 4 before taking action.

When communicating your anger, you'll have the highest chance of success if you wait until you can talk about your emotions without getting overly emotional. Mollie gets angry when doctors refuse to admit that they don't know something. She has now learned to say calmly, "It will be more helpful to me if you are honest and tell me you don't know why I still have pain and when the pain will go away. I know that many patients don't like to hear this, but for me the truth is better." Mollie found that communicating her needs at the start of an appointment made the rest of the conversation go much more smoothly.

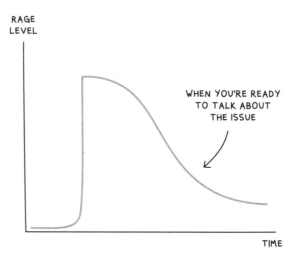

RAGE LEVEL

WHEN YOU'RE READY TO TALK ABOUT THE ISSUE

TIME

If your anger was triggered by someone else's anger, you may want to share how their actions affected you. While we (Liz and Mollie) were leading a workshop, a woman asked what to do when her boss yelled at her. Another participant spoke up. "I am an executive assistant, and my boss used to frequently yell at me," she told the group. "Even when he wasn't angry at me but was angry about something else. It would make me flustered, and then frustrated that he was making me flustered. One day I finally said to him, 'I know that you're upset right now, but when you yell at me, I'm not able to focus on my work.'" Her boss apologized and realized that he was inadvertently hurting her performance. His outbursts became much less frequent.

We recommend asking yourself these four questions before you communicate your anger:

- What is my goal?
- What can I say to achieve that goal?
- How should I say it?
- When should I say it?[39]

Sometimes, you'll have to face the ugly truth that you're angry because of something you can't change—or because of something that you *might* be able to change but can't take on in the moment. Other times, the person who hurt you won't admit to having caused you pain. In those instances, look for ways to remove yourself from the situation or, if you can't walk away, to indirectly address your needs.

After being harassed in the elevator, Griffin consulted with his parents and LGBTQ activists. He ultimately decided not to bring a case forward. But that didn't mean he was going to stay at the company. Griffin spent a month getting up at 2 A.M. to take job interviews with employers in other time zones. "I masked anger with hyperactivity," he told us. Nearly a decade later, at the urging of his fiancé, he shared his story publicly as an encouraging demonstration of solidarity.

Or take reader Rachel, who felt powerless in the face of a difficult boss but couldn't quit their job right away. "His unrealistic expectations and authoritarian leadership style left me in a constant cycle of stress and inadequacy," they told us. Rachel started to take small steps to boost their self-confidence and feel more valued at work. First, they reduced how much they interacted with their boss. "I also built a network of mentors and colleagues who knew me and appreciated me in ways my boss didn't. That helped me prevent his feedback from sabotaging my self-worth."[40]

GIVE YOURSELF PERMISSION TO BE ANGRY

TAKE SOME TIME TO COOL DOWN

ANGER TIP JAR

EXPLORE WHAT MADE YOU SO UPSET

FIGURE OUT A WAY TO ADDRESS YOUR NEEDS

Expressing your anger

For many years, Mollie made a point of avoiding being perceived as frustrated. Whether she was emailing a client or talking to her landlord, she would say things like "I'm sure you didn't mean it like this" or "I would love it if you'd do ____, but no rush!"

After researching anger for this chapter, Mollie began to experiment with more direct communication. She made sure to never be rude, but she dropped niceties and qualifiers. She started saying,

"Our lights are flickering. When can you send someone to fix it?" or "I disagree with this research conclusion. What did you base it on?" Adopting a more direct communication style may make some people uncomfortable, but that's not the end of the world. It's a powerful way to more clearly communicate what you are thinking and feeling.

Many of us never learned how to talk about our anger using specific vocabulary. But improving our ability to talk about intense emotions is beneficial to our mental and physical health. Neuroscientist Matthew Lieberman found that translating emotions into specific language frees up our brain from dwelling on negative emotions. And research "shows that people who openly express their feelings are healthier than those who habitually suppress strong emotions."[41]

To practice expressing your anger, try journaling about your emotions—without using the word *angry*. Instead, use other words that may better describe your specific emotions. A few examples:

- displeasure
- dissatisfaction
- annoyance
- frustration
- powerlessness
- rage
- exasperation
- resentment
- indignation
- *Backpfeifengesicht*—a German word that roughly means "a face in need of a slap"

- *huǐhèn*—a Mandarin Chinese word for anger directed toward yourself
- *kankan*—a Japanese onomatopoeic word that describes both furious anger and the blaze of something red-hot
- *hi fun kou gai*—a Japanese compound meaning indignation about the wickedness of the world or directed at an unchangeable situation
- *dépité*—a French adjective that combines disappointment and irritation[42]

5. Channel your anger energy strategically

For a long time, Rutgers professor Dr. Brittney Cooper thought she needed to be in control of her emotions to be respected—and to avoid being labeled as an "angry Black woman." But that changed when one of her students told her, "I love to listen to you lecture because your lectures [are] filled with . . . the most eloquent rage."[43] The authenticity of Dr. Cooper's emotion made her students pay attention. Now she thinks of anger as "a superpower" that can give Black women "the strength to fight injustice and to imagine and build new worlds."

Anger can be a powerful tool for change, at both an individual and a societal level. Ever heard "Don't get mad; get even"? We like to say, "Use your mad to get even."

Rage can clarify the kind of world we want to live in. "Movements come from anger," says clinical psychologist Dr. Lina Perl. "Instead of an individual expressing her need or setting a boundary, it's a group of people setting a boundary."[44] Take the Me Too movement, which was a direct result of women's anger. After actress Ashley Judd publicly accused the film producer Harvey Weinstein of sexual harassment, many women came forward with similar experiences. They were motivated by their own anger, and their anger on behalf of one another and their collective pain. The fear that fed their silence could only have been overcome by anger.

After the Ku Klux Klan bombed a Baptist church in Birmingham, Alabama, in 1963, singer Nina Simone was so angry, she said, "I had it in mind to go out and kill someone." Her husband encouraged her to channel her anger into what she did best. She wrote the song "Mississippi Goddam," which became one of the best-known protest songs of the civil rights era.[45]

If we tap into it, anger can actually increase our confidence and make us certain that we are capable and strong.[46] Researchers have found that people who are angry also hold the belief that they will prevail under any circumstances.[47] During US Navy SEAL training, new recruits learn that they can use the intense emotions and adrenaline that come from rage to give them energy when they face dangerous circumstances.[48] You can use this same strategy to use anger as the motivation to effectively advocate for yourself. Say you feel you deserve a promotion but have been scared to ask for it. Think to yourself: What would I do if I were the type of person who got angry about this? Or what would I suggest that a friend do in this situation if I were angry on their behalf?

Anger has also been shown to boost creativity. "All innovation comes from fury," writes author Tom Peters. When we're mad at the old, we're driven to invent the new.[49] Pixar executive Brad Bird intentionally recruited frustrated animators to work on a new film because he believed they were most likely to change things for the better.[50] The result? *The Incredibles*, a movie that broke box office records.

• • •

Most of us are raised to equate anger with out-of-control meltdowns. But anger is an important signal that something is wrong. And, harnessed effectively, it can give us the strength we need to make things right. By pinpointing why you're suddenly sobbing tears of frustration alone in your car, you can figure out what to do next, and eventually move to a healthier, happier place.

TAKEAWAYS

* Anger is evolution's alarm bell; listen to what it's telling you
* Biases and stereotypes often cloud our judgment of who is angry
* Figure out your triggers to reduce future flare-ups
* Understand your expression style to better communicate your feelings
* Allow yourself to be upset, and then pinpoint the needs behind your emotion
* Address your needs, either directly or indirectly
* Use anger as fuel to drive change or spark creativity

CHAPTER 4

Burnout

I thought burnout was like a cold you catch and recover from—
which is why I missed the diagnosis altogether.

Anne Helen Petersen

MOLLIE: *I remember reading, in my late twenties, about how TV writer Joey Soloway had an idea for a bumper sticker that said* DOWNTIME MAKES ME ANXIOUS[1] *and thinking with pride, "ME TOO!! Look at all these people who come home and just watch TV at night." I had my evenings and weekends booked out for months. Being busy was my specialty, despite the fact that I was an introvert and homebody at heart. Because I was initiating most of my busyness, I thought I was immune from burnout-based exhaustion.*

But before I tell you about my complete meltdown, let me tell you about what led to the crash. On December 23, 2018, I was sitting in a first-class cabin, flying home to Seattle for the holidays. I was only in first class because, during the previous three months, I had flown back and forth between New York City and Montreal for a client project every week (I was working as a consultant for global innovation firm IDEO at the time) . . . plus a quick trip to Shanghai for a work meeting . . . PLUS a weekend trip to DC to do a leadership-coach training workshop. I looked around at everyone else in first class and noticed their faces straining to work on their laptops in the darkness of the cabin. Their expressions matched what I was feeling: exhaustion coupled with an addictive adrenaline from new emails coming in, projects to comment on, and chat messages to answer. My decades of envy for those in first class had vanished. If you are in first class because of how many miles you have flown, your life is out of balance, whether you admit it or not.

*The person next to me on the plane started coughing, and I imme-
diately covered my face with my scarf and turned away. I couldn't get
sick. I had so much to do before our book launch at the end of January,
plus I had holiday parties to attend. I was already planning to take
two weeks off for our book tour, so I'd feel guilty if I missed more work
that month because I was sick. My breakneck pace was costing me the
ability to take care of my body and take the rest I needed.*

*I shut my laptop and listened to a podcast to block out the anxiety.
I figured I had a week off in front of me, and that would alleviate all
the stress, right?*

• • •

M any books, articles, and experts describe burnout as if it's solely related to how much we work—and suggest that if we take time off, we'll soon bounce back, born anew. But a vacation will not cure burnout.

Burnout isn't only about the hours you're putting in. It's also a function of the stories you tell yourself and how you approach what you do—in the office *and* at home. In fact, people who quit their jobs often find themselves, six months later, in a different role but feeling similarly depleted.

Burnout, a chronic feeling of exhaustion and stress, is on the rise. In fact, it's become so pervasive that in 2019, it was officially recognized as a diagnosable condition in the United States (see page 215 for the Burnout Profile Assessment).[2] In 2020, more than 70 percent of employees experienced burnout at least once.[3] And a national survey of college students found that a whopping 87 percent felt overwhelmed by everything they had to do.[4]

At its core, burnout is a symptom of capitalism. Mollie's father often reminds her that because she was born in the late eighties, after the embrace of Reagan supply-side economics and deinstitutionalization, she can't comprehend what it feels like to live in a society with a real safety net. Mollie imagines she would feel

WHAT BURNOUT FEELS LIKE

WORK
NONSTOP

PANIC ABOUT ALL
THE WORK YOU
STILL HAVE LEFT

PANIC ABOUT ALL
THE WORK YOU
STILL HAVE LEFT

TRY TO TAKE
A BREAK

much less stressed if her health insurance, retirement plan, and ability to pay for her mortgage and any future children's education didn't rely solely on her ability to work as many hours as she possibly can for the highest hourly wage, because these are her income-generating, child-free years. (Deep breath!)

And just as the benefits of capitalism tend to accrue unevenly along lines of income level, gender, and race, so, too, does the burden of burnout. The stresses of working a minimum-wage job and living paycheck to paycheck are extreme causes of burnout. So is surface acting, when you feel like you have to suppress your true emotions to fit in or be heard while contending with blatant discrimination.[5] Unsurprisingly, women and people of color are much more likely to experience burnout than their male, white counterparts.[6] "Burnout is something that is inculcated into the way that Black women live life," explains Kelly Pierre-Louisa, a Black marketing executive and entrepreneur. "Because we have so much on our shoulders, we push our personal well-being to the back of our minds."[7]

Given all those structural forces, isn't a manager, CEO, or elected official the only one who can really cure your burnout? Larger changes to our job and life situations would certainly help. A lot. To that end, we've included a section in this chapter on page 113 on how managers and leaders can better support their people.

But waiting on someone else to solve your burnout takes time and (unfortunately) isn't guaranteed. That's why we'll spend most of this chapter focusing on what you can do now to feel better. That involves examining and adjusting your internal narratives, uncoupling your worth from what you do, and setting better boundaries for yourself. We'll offer you immediate relief by busting common myths around burnout and then help you move forward in a sustainable way so you prioritize yourself.

A note: We'll talk about burnout largely in the context of work, but we use that word liberally. There are many types of work: your job, caring for your loved ones (anthropologists call this *kinwork*), showing up for your friends, and taking care of yourself. The advice we share is intended to be helpful in addressing burnout across each of these domains.

MYTHS ABOUT BURNOUT

Myth #1: Burnout is obvious

We think we'll be able to tell when our brains are fried. But staying afloat while fielding a firestorm of notifications and hurtling from one meeting to the next can be so emotionally consuming that we don't even realize the extent of our fatigue. That's why burnout often seems sudden: it's the crash after you've been unknowingly running on empty for too long.

One of the most dangerous aspects of burnout is that it impacts self-awareness. When you're in it, you're fueled by adrenaline, and the momentum feels so exhilarating that you end up adding more and more to your plate. It wasn't until Mollie got sick and then injured (more on that later) that she looked back and realized, "Oh god, why did I make myself do all of that?" But she didn't *feel* on the verge of burnout at the time. She felt like a superwoman.

Once burnout hits, it can take weeks or even months to overcome. So what early signs should you look out for? Here are some of the subtle cues indicating that you might need to reassess how much you're taking on:

- Basic activities like going to the grocery store feel overstimulating
- You feel so overwhelmed that you've started to cut out activities you know are good for you (such as exercise or alone time)
- You have the Sunday scaries—on Saturday
- You're saying yes even though you're already at capacity
- You feel like you're running purely on fumes
- You find everyone and everything irritating
- Getting sick and being forced to shut down for a bit sounds kind of nice
- You're suffering from Groundhog Day Syndrome: every day starts to feel the same
- You're all too familiar with "revenge bedtime procrastination," when you stubbornly stay up late because you didn't get any time to yourself during the day[8]

We're quick to ignore these signs, because we can usually muscle through them. But they're important alarm bells. As Naveed Ahmad, the founder of Flourish, a company that helps people combat burnout, told us, "Sometimes life taps you on the shoulder with a feather, sometimes it hits you with a brick, and sometimes it runs you over with a bus. Learn to listen when it's just a feather."

Myth #2: Addressing burnout isn't urgent if you're not falling apart

Recalling a time when he was shuttling his terminally ill dad between appointments while struggling with his own addiction, actor Dax Shepard reflected, "I didn't realize until much later it was stressful. In the moment, I was

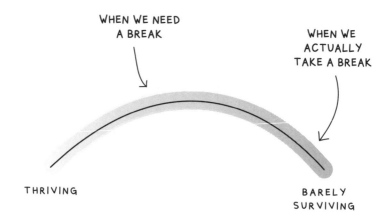

WHEN WE NEED
A BREAK

WHEN WE
ACTUALLY
TAKE A BREAK

THRIVING

BARELY
SURVIVING

distracted by logistics. And I could control the logistics, so I just told myself everything was fine."[9]

We tend to believe that as long as we're able to put one foot in front of the other, there's no need for concern or rest. So we keep pushing and pushing: we schedule a client meeting during our lunch break, we drag ourselves out of bed at the crack of dawn to join an international call, we feel responsible for extinguishing every fire at work and at home. On their own, these personal violations may be small. But as Dr. Richard Gunderman writes, burnout "is the sum total of hundreds and thousands of tiny betrayals of purpose, each one so minute that it hardly attracts notice."[10]

Technology has normalized operating at a breakneck pace. Studies show we check our emails an average of seventy-four times a day and switch tasks *every three minutes.*[11] (How many times have you checked your phone since starting this chapter?) Our "always on" habits mean our minds are never quiet, and we feel frantic when we try to disconnect. So we keep moving at a speed that prevents reflection and rest.

When we ricochet from one thing to the next, we accumulate stress in our bodies. In their book *Burnout*, Drs. (and sisters) Emily and Amelia Nagoski write that when our ancestors were faced with a predator, they would either work with others to slay the beast or flee: the fight-or-flight response. Doing so required

1	2	3	4	5	6	7
FIND TIME TO RELAX TOMORROW	FIND TIME TO RELAX TOMORROW	FIND TIME TO RELAX TOMORROW	FIND TIME TO RELAX TOMORROW	FIND TIME TO RELAX TOMORROW	FIND TIME TO RELAX TOMORROW	FIND TIME TO RELAX TOMORROW
8	**9**	**10**	**11**	**12**	**13**	**14**
FIND TIME TO RELAX TOMORROW	FIND TIME TO RELAX TOMORROW	FIND TIME TO RELAX TOMORROW	FIND TIME TO RELAX TOMORROW	FIND TIME TO RELAX TOMORROW	FIND TIME TO RELAX TOMORROW	FIND TIME TO RELAX TOMORROW
15	**16**	**17**	**18**	**19**	**20**	**21**
FIND TIME TO RELAX TOMORROW	FIND TIME TO RELAX TOMORROW	FIND TIME TO RELAX TOMORROW	FIND TIME TO RELAX TOMORROW	FIND TIME TO RELAX TOMORROW	FIND TIME TO RELAX TOMORROW	FIND TIME TO RELAX TOMORROW
22	**23**	**24**	**25**	**26**	**27**	**28**
FIND TIME TO RELAX TOMORROW	FIND TIME TO RELAX TOMORROW	FIND TIME TO RELAX TOMORROW	FIND TIME TO RELAX TOMORROW	FIND TIME TO RELAX TOMORROW	FIND TIME TO RELAX TOMORROW	FIND TIME TO RELAX TOMORROW
29	**30**					
FIND TIME TO RELAX TOMORROW	FIND TIME TO RELAX TOMORROW					

them to draw on what's called *surge capacity*: the set of adaptive systems (a rush of adrenaline, a pounding heartbeat) humans rely on to react to an emergency.[12] But surge capacity lasts only so long, and our ancestors used it only in short bursts, to escape death. When they successfully survived, they felt exhilarated and could then relax again. And so the stress cycle would be completed.[13]

In the modern world, we operate on surge capacity *all the time*, because we never complete the stress cycle. If you're stuck in traffic for hours, you won't immediately feel better as you walk through your front door. Your body will still be in the middle of a stress response. And if you haven't made it a habit to go for a walk or wind down, you will continue to produce the stress hormone cortisol for the rest of the evening.[14] Eventually, all that accumulated stress will catch up to you and you'll crash. (For ways to complete the stress cycle, see "Get comfortable living at 80 percent" on page 97.)

Myth #3: Everyone's burnout is the same

Burnout has become an umbrella term. When we spoke with readers, they used it to mean they were tired, bored, fed up with their managers, overwhelmed by personal responsibilities, depressed, working too many hours—the list goes on and on. In other words, there are many shades of burnout. It's useful to understand exactly what you're feeling so you can get the specific support that will be most helpful. If you feel fried because you're pulling long hours, that has different implications than if you work from nine to five but are depressed because you find your role meaningless.

The Maslach Burnout Inventory (MBI)—the first clinically based measure of burnout, created by psychologist Christina Maslach—looks at three dimensions of burnout:

1. Exhaustion: you feel constantly depleted
2. Cynicism: you feel detached from your job and the people around you
3. Ineffectiveness: you feel that you're never able to do a good enough job

The MBI is often misinterpreted (and we understand why—it's complicated!). People tend to focus solely on exhaustion, or add the scores from each dimension and assume there is a clear boundary between "not burned out" and "burned out."[15] But, as Maslach explains, there is no arbitrary dividing point. Instead, your scores on each dimension place you in one of five profiles that sit on a continuum between the most positive experience, feeling engaged, and the least, feeling burned out.

To help you better understand what you're feeling, we've included our adaptation of the MBI assessment, the Burnout Profile Assessment, on page 215. Once you've taken it, write down your score for each dimension and then use the following list to identify which of the five profiles on the burnout continuum best represents your experience.

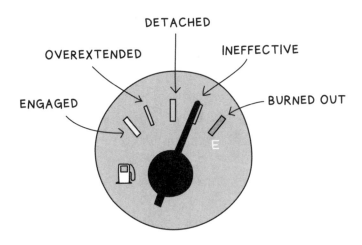

Five Profiles on the Burnout Continuum, from Most to Least Positive

1. **Engaged:** low-to-moderate degree of **exhaustion** and **cynicism**, moderate-to-high degree of **effectiveness**
   - You're doing pretty well, or at least okay.
2. **Overextended:** high degree of **exhaustion**
   - Everything feels overwhelming, and you're overworked. Feeling overextended is often the result of having too much work or being in an always-on work culture. But it can also happen when you have taken on too many side projects or have time-consuming health issues or family obligations.
3. **Disengaged:** high degree of **cynicism**
   - You don't feel connected to your colleagues, and you lack empathy for those around you. We often become disengaged when we're overdoing it, or when we no longer feel that what we do matters.
4. **Ineffective:** high degree of **ineffectiveness**
   - You feel incompetent and unproductive. You may actually be effective at your job, but your perception is that you are ineffective.

5. **Burned out:** high degree of **exhaustion** and **cynicism**, low degree of **effectiveness**

- You are beyond tired—you're discouraged and alienated.[16] Mollie experienced complete burnout in late 2018 and early 2019. She was **overextended**, felt **disengaged** from her colleagues, and thought she was **ineffective** both at IDEO and at helping launch our book *No Hard Feelings*.

• • •

MOLLIE: *When I returned to New York at the end of December 2018, I got a bad cold. My body had simply had enough. However, my husband and I had plans to travel over the Martin Luther King holiday weekend, and my cold was almost better. But it turns out that flying when not fully recovered is a terrible idea. On the flight back, I picked up the flu and could not get off the couch for a week.*

I lay comatose, cursing myself for taking the trip, but the bullet train of the life I had designed for myself wasn't about to stop. For our book launch, I was supposed to go to London, then back to New York, then to San Francisco for events.

At the urging of Liz and our agent, I canceled the London trip. But I couldn't let go of the guilt. What would happen to our book if I missed more events? What would my colleagues think of me, now that I had been sick for two weeks and was planning to take more time off? As often happens during burnout, the questions start small and get larger and more existential. They shift from logistical questions into questions about our fears and beliefs: Why was I living in a city that stressed me out? Why was I trying to write a book and work a full-time job at the same time?

As Mary Pipher writes, "Many people politely fall apart at some point in their lives. . . . Recovery requires the building of a roomier container"in which to live our lives. I thought that I just had to work harder at managing stress, but really, I needed a container that had more downtime and room for bigger questions. I also had to get comfortable with what that roominess felt like.[17]

HOW TO WORK THROUGH IT

Overcoming burnout requires regular checkups. In this section, we'll help you understand how to alleviate or prevent burnout based on the profile you identified in the previous section. We'll also cover what managers and teams can do to help their people find better balance.

1. What to do if you are overextended

GET COMFORTABLE LIVING AT 80 PERCENT

To study burnout, researcher Melissa Gregg interviewed exhausted knowledge workers at four organizations over the course of three years. To her surprise, all of them attributed their job-related fatigue to some sort of personal failure. No one thought that they might just be overworked.[18]

If you feel constantly depleted, chances are your days are filled with back-to-back obligations and stressful deadlines. How much of that is self-inflicted? We've been there. We used to (and sometimes still do, to be honest) go above and beyond *on everything*, even when it wasn't necessary. During slow periods at work, Liz would frantically assign herself a bunch of nonurgent, nonimportant tasks. And when Mollie, an introvert who loves cozy nights in, saw an empty evening on her calendar, she would immediately book another dinner or event. In both cases, we would have been better served by giving ourselves a break.

If everything is running smoothly, piling your plate with to-dos can work. But then you get sick, or have to support a family member, or your boss quits, and suddenly you go from 100 to 120 percent and your life melts into an unmanageable nightmare.

To become more of a tortoise than a hare, we encourage you to get comfortable living at 80 percent. (Do not confuse this advice with the suggestion to work 80 percent time for 80 percent salary. This rarely works out; you will end up working full time but getting paid for only 80 percent of your hours.) Reader Ellie told us that after one of her family members became terminally ill, she forced herself to slow down. "This has been as simple as prioritizing exercise, not opening my work computer after 6 P.M., and allowing myself to read whatever sounds fun, as opposed to what I think I 'should' read."

This might take practice. When our friend Miriam, an engineer, felt overworked, her psychiatrist asked if she'd ever stopped in the middle of working on something—and just walked away. "I hadn't," Miriam told us. "He told me to try. I experimented with this the next day at work. At five thirty, I stood up from my desk and went home. When I came back to work the next day, nothing was on fire." Miriam now regularly pauses her work when she feels tired or her hands start to hurt. And every time, it's fine.[19]

You may also find it helpful to place a part of your life on the back burner at times. When Liz's dad was in the hospital, she cut back on social events for a while. And when reader Paul was diagnosed with Crohn's disease, he decided to put off trying to get promoted for a bit while he worked on his health. This idea has come to be known as the Four Burners Theory, for a story author David Sedaris once related in a *New Yorker* article. A friend (who was passing on the story from a management seminar she'd attended) told him that your life has four burners: family, friends, health, and work. To be successful, you need to have one of the burners off at all times. And to be *really* successful, you have to shut off two.[20]

Living at 80 percent will also give you natural breaks, during which you can complete the stress cycle. Pause, and tune in to your body. "Your body tells you everything you need to know, but [you have] to learn to listen," Beyoncé told *Harper's Bazaar.*[21] According to the Nagoski sisters, there are seven ways to listen to your body and break the stress cycle:

- Cry
- Take slow, deep breaths (Mollie likes to do breathing exercises; see the "List of favorite guided meditations" on pages 233–34.)
- Do a physical activity (Liz likes to replace mental exhaustion with physical exhaustion; she finds that an hour on the elliptical machine at the end of each day makes a world of difference.)
- Laugh
- Hang out with friends
- Do something creative, like write or draw
- Engage in physical affection, like asking for a hug[22]

LEARN TO DRAW—AND RESPECT—YOUR OWN LINES

Here's the thing: you have to set and stick to your own boundaries. No one else is going to draw them for you. You may sometimes wonder: Why don't the people who love me help me not overdo it? Often, it's because they want you to be

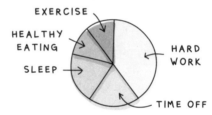

successful! And a marker of success in our society is being busy. They may be just as busy as you are. Or they may not know what your boundaries are. In *Set Boundaries, Find Peace*, Nedra Glover Tawwab writes, "People don't know what you want. It's your job to make it clear. Clarity saves relationships."[23]

It takes courage to say no and stick to it without feeling guilty. The next time you're on the brink of saying yes to something you're not excited about, pause. Ask yourself:

- If I say yes, what do I gain?
- If I do this, what will I *not* be able to do instead?
- If I say no, what's the worst thing that would happen?

Behind every no is a deeper yes, even if that yes is just to yourself. Reader Kylie told us that during a time when she had a lot of family commitments, she became much more deliberate about what she took on at work. "What will it mean for my family if I volunteer to do this?" she would ask herself. "How important is it really? And at what cost?" That helped her reduce the amount of "mindless urgency and activity" in her life.[24]

Once you're ready to move forward with a no, come up with two phrases: one to say to the other person, and one to say to yourself. For example, when you decline an invitation from a friend, you might say, "I'd love to, but I'm not free this week. How about later in the month?" and tell yourself, "Saying no to this right now does not make me a bad friend. It makes me a human who needs rest." Your phrase for the other person can also just be a simple, "I can't, sorry!" The word *no* is also a complete sentence.

IMPORTANT LINES TO DRAW

Liz struggled with saying no until she created a set of rules that she can reference. Now she'll say, "I have a rule that I don't book social events on Thursday nights," or "I have a rule that I always sleep on it before making a commitment." She's found that people tend to take a no less personally when it's tied to a rule. "People respect rules, and they accept that it's not you rejecting the offer, request, demand, or opportunity, but the rule allows you no choice," writes author Ryan Holiday.[25]

Your capacity is also going to be different from everyone else's. Your friends, your coworkers, and even your partner may not share your burnout triggers. For example, if you're an introvert and your partner is an extrovert, they may see you in a slump and encourage you to schedule dinner with friends or go to a show. That's what *they* would do to feel better. But that might be the exact opposite of what restores you. Mollie's husband, a comedian and TV writer, had his own regrets about turning down opportunities that, in retrospect, might have been career-changing. So he heavily encouraged Mollie to go to London and not miss out on what he saw as a "once-in-a-lifetime opportunity," even though she was sick and she did not share his career goals.

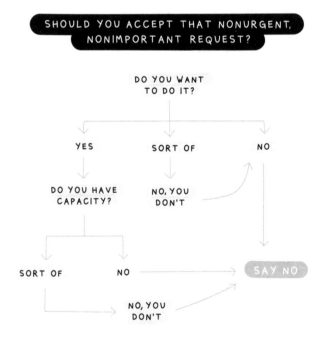

When does burnout mean you should leave your job?

By now, you might be thinking: "Okay, sure, I can take steps to combat burnout, but isn't there a point when it's time to throw in the towel and quit my job?" Yes, there is.

Several people we spoke with about burnout told us that they only felt better once they'd left an unhealthy work environment. As a consultant, reader Maike battled constant anxiety despite getting promoted and receiving positive performance reviews. "Because I was performing well, I thought my mental health would improve at some point." But after she switched to a job in an industry that was less fast-paced and stressful, her anxiety disappeared. "I always thought it was 90 percent me, 10 percent environment," she told us. "But I was wrong."[26]

If you've applied most of the advice we offer in this chapter and you're still fighting a losing battle, that's a strong signal it's time to get out. And that's okay. It doesn't make you weak or ungrateful or someone who "couldn't stand the heat." Many of us are part of what writer Connie Wang calls the "grateful to be here" generation.[27] But sacrificing your health and potentially your self-worth should not be the price you have to pay to participate.

As you start looking for new roles, we encourage you to reflect on why you're unhappy in your current job—and what you need to feel better in your next one. Without a clear sense of what kind of changes would help you, you're likely to find yourself in the same emotional place, just at a different job. Try answering these questions:

* What would it take for me to be happy in my current position? Is that possible?
* What aspects of my work environment contribute to my burnout?
* What scares me about leaving my job? How real are those fears?

Finally, don't rush. Make sure that you leave for a role that is more suited to your needs so you don't end up in the same situation.

2. What to do if you are disengaged

SEEK OUT CONNECTIONS

This takes effort, we know. When you're tired and cynical, you usually lack the energy to reach out. But isolating yourself kicks off a vicious cycle: you don't invest in connection when you need it most, which means you're left alone to dwell on your exhaustion, and you end up feeling even more depleted.

When Mollie was traveling a lot for work, she started to feel disengaged from her IDEO colleagues back in New York. She missed the casual interactions and check-ins that came with being in the office. She had some work friends—but she didn't know them well enough to invite them to do something on the weekend. Eventually, she had had enough. Although it was anxiety-inducing, she decided to invite fourteen of them over for an afternoon. The risk paid off; everyone had fun, so they got together a couple more times. These gatherings made it easier for Mollie to build individual friendships, since she had a chance to get to know everyone first in a group setting.

You don't need to make a new best friend to feel better; even small moments of connection go far. In a study, researchers told cynical people to focus on helping others for the day. The participants begrudgingly took small actions, like giving people kudos for their efforts or going to lunch with a couple co-workers. The following morning, the group reported lower levels of cynicism.[28] Here are a few small ways you can seek connection:

- Set up a time with a colleague to grab coffee or catch up on a video call
- Go for a walk-and-talk
- Invite a friend over just to sit on your couch and chat
- Thank someone who recently helped you

That said, be thoughtful about whom you reach out to. An important part of reducing your cynicism is to keep a distance from people or situations you find frustrating and draining. "When I hit a wall at work, I made it a point to spend more time with considerate colleagues," reader Edwin told us, "and to avoid this one program manager I couldn't stand. That made a world of difference."

RECONNECT WITH MEANING—AND THEN REBUILD YOUR ROUTINES

Another way to rekindle your connection with what you do is to ask yourself: Why am I doing this?

Meaning can take many forms. We spoke with a doctor who starts every day by reminding herself of the impact she can have on her patients' lives; an engineer who told us she feels a sense of purpose when she's able to automate something to make life easier for her colleagues; and a lawyer who said that on his hardest days he focuses on the pride he feels for being able to provide for his family.

If you're having trouble coming up with anything specific, try tracking what you do and how it makes you feel for a week. Liz once spent ten days carefully updating a spreadsheet with what she did every hour and how she felt on a scale of 1 (drained) to 10 (excited). Her data showed she was most miserable on days with back-to-back meetings and happiest during periods when she had a few hours set aside for deep work and ample alone time. She now makes it a point to spread out her meetings and social hangouts, block off time on her calendar for focused work, and keep a few evenings per week free for herself.

Figuring out what you *don't* find meaningful can be just as useful as identifying what you enjoy doing. If there are specific people or activities that frustrate you, see if you can shift your life away from them. Psychologists often talk about *job crafting*, when you take proactive steps and actions to redesign what you do at work. We encourage you to life craft. What or who makes you feel valued? Can you invest more in those areas and people? What nonessential activities make you feel stressed out? Can you take those off your plate?

3. What to do if you are feeling ineffective

SWAP BEING REACTIVE WITH BEING PROACTIVE

When you feel ineffective, it's usually due to one of three reasons: you don't have enough time to do everything that's expected of you, you lack enough context to make informed decisions, or you're not supported and recognized by the people around you.

Many readers told us they felt like they were "never done" and were running in circles, "constantly responding to requests." It's hard to maintain your confidence—or feel anything close to a sense of accomplishment—if you're only reacting. This usually also means you're working on such a disparate set of projects that you lose sense of the bigger picture.

First, shed the notion that to be a good employee (or friend or spouse or mom), you need to respond to every single request. We love writer Jenna Wortham's advice: "Remember that other people's urgency is not your emergency."[29] Part of your role is to set reasonable expectations. "A lot of times, what clients label a crisis is not actually one," Barbara, the CEO of a PR firm, told *Harvard Business Review*. She recommends finding ways to kindly but firmly put things into perspective for others.[30] Try these phrases to do that:

- Here's how I think we could do this with the least disruption.
- I understand you want _____. I'm currently doing _____, and I have these concerns about _____. Can we talk about what the best next steps might be?
- Here's what I'm currently working on. Let me know which tasks you think could help with_____. Then I can try to prioritize those.

And remember: your achievable goals don't have to be work-related. "I went through a period in my job where I felt like I was running through a maze blindfolded," reader Jess told us. "There was very little structure to my projects, and the goals kept changing, so the work felt never-ending." Jess decided to take a beginner's wheel-throwing pottery class that met on Monday and Wednesday evenings. It forced her to leave the office at a reasonable hour and helped her regain confidence in her ability to learn and progress. "When you first start something, you make really fast, measurable, and noticeable improvements," she told us. "I needed that."

FIGURE OUT WHY YOUR EFFORT DOESN'T FEEL WORTH IT

MAKE SURE YOU'RE EXCITED ABOUT THIS PART, TOO

IF YOU'RE GOING TO SPEND A LOT OF TIME HERE

"Feeling burned out is less about overwork and more about the ineffectiveness of work," tweeted Facebook product manager Dare Obasanjo. "It's not enough to take a break[; you also need] to examine why your subconscious thinks the effort you're putting in isn't worth it."[31]

If you're consistently feeling a lack of achievement, it might also be time to take a step back and get clear on what you value. It doesn't matter how quickly you climb a ladder if you don't care about what's at the top.

Take a look at the "List of values" we pulled together on pages 234–35 and identify the five that are most important to you. Liz most values autonomy, creativity, kindness, recognition, and success, while Mollie's list is community, creativity, learning, contribution, and self-respect. Then ask yourself:

- Does your work align with those values?
- Does what you do in your free time align with those values?

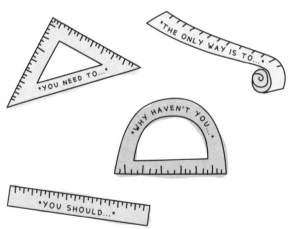

Setting priorities involves picking some things over others. There's a story about a professor filling a jar with large marbles. "Is the jar full?" he asks his class. "Yes," they respond. He adds pebbles and shakes the jar so they fill the crevices. "Is the jar full?" "Yes." Finally, he pours in sand. "Is the jar full?" The students look at the stuffed jar and laugh. "In the jar that is your life, the marbles are what's most important: your well-being, your important relationships. The pebbles represent other things that matter, like work and school. The sand is the small things that seem significant in the moment, like material possessions. But," the professor says, "if you fill your jar with sand first, by prioritizing the little things over what's most important, you won't have room left for what matters."

We often only realize we need to make a change when we achieve a lofty goal but don't feel excited about it. In 2012, our friend Naveed finally got the big promotion he had been working toward for years. But his euphoria quickly faded. Just a few days later, he was miserable again.

That weekend, Naveed created a Google document titled "Who Am I?" and wrote down the values he wanted to live by. "I unconditionally give my best self to others," he typed out. "I am better than my previous self." "I care for my body, mind, and soul." Once he was finished, he went back and highlighted every item he didn't feel he was living by in red. That day, most of the list was red.

Naveed then took steps to build a life for himself that more closely aligned with his aspirational values. He found a new job that was more personally meaningful, started to make exercise and meditation a more consistent part of his routine, and prioritized his personal relationships over work. From time to time, he'll go through his list again to remind himself of the life he wants to be living. If he's gotten better at living by one of the values, he'll change it from red to black. "That always comes with a sense of relief and calm," he told us.[32]

4. What to do if you are completely burned out

DETACH YOUR WORTH FROM WHAT YOU DO

"You are not the work you do; you are the person you are," writes the author Toni Morrison.[33] We would add: your work won't love you back.

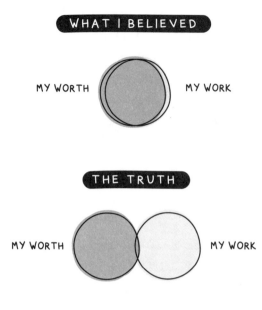

Loving your work is wonderful, but there are limits. When two individuals lose their separate identities in each other, psychologists call it *enmeshment*. The same can happen when you tie your self-worth too closely to your output or to a specific identity.[34] When this happens, you start to lose sight of other important parts of yourself and your mental well-being becomes overly wrapped up in achieving your goals.

Many readers shared with us that they were suffering profoundly because of burnout but that they felt their sense of self was so tied up in their output that to change anything would feel like jumping off a cliff. We heard about people going to the office bathroom because it was the only place they could take a breather, getting weekly migraines from staying late at work, and collapsing in the office parking lot.

If you are experiencing deep enmeshment, sometimes the only way to decouple your identity from what you do is to stop. Reader Lisa cried almost every day during her last year as a school principal in Denver. "I was so emotionally exhausted," she told us. "I was also grasping for validation. I became hooked on things like Peloton as a way to collect evidence that I was successful at something—even if I felt defeated in every other dimension." Lisa ended up quitting her job as principal, despite having no defined plan for what would come next. While navigating her transition, she went to grad school, and she credits this time as an important part of rebuilding her identity. Lisa thinks it can be powerful to stop and create space to redefine yourself outside your title or role—which might mean stepping away from your current job for a bit.

But quitting or taking a break isn't always an option. If you're exhausted, you can't financially leave, or you need to stay to get promoted to a job you do want, the best thing to do is to invest in your life outside of work—and to lower your expectations of your work self. In the summer of 2020, in the midst of the COVID pandemic, Liz was helping her husband take care of his father, who was dying of cancer. Up to that point, Liz had always prided herself on going above and beyond at her job and getting everything done ahead of schedule. But by August, Liz was waking up every morning in a mix of panic and dread and found it hard to focus at work. Everything felt like a mountain she didn't have the energy to climb, whether it was giving a big customer presentation or just replying to a text from a friend. Liz remembers her husband asking her if she could send him a Google Calendar invite for a date night and feeling like she couldn't handle even that tiny request.

Liz finally put her work on the back burner for a while. She took two weeks of vacation and, when she went back to work, made a point of doing a "good enough" job for a bit. She would finish everything that needed to be done but stopped working at 5:30 P.M., deleted Slack from her phone, and didn't take on any additional big projects for the month. It helped. Just giving herself the grace to not be the best at work all the time helped her feel better.

MAKE TIME FOR GARBAGE TIME

When bestselling author Brené Brown was working on her first book, her husband took the kids to visit his mother so Brené could have a three-day weekend to herself to write a chapter draft. When he got back, he asked her, "Did you get a lot of work done?"

"I watched forty-six episodes of *Law & Order*," Brené admitted.

YOU SHOULD PROBABLY TAKE ONE

A REAL BREAK · A REAL BREAK · A REAL BREAK · A REAL BREAK · A REAL BREAK · A REAL BREAK

She and her husband got into a tense argument. But three days later, on Thursday night, Brené finished the chapter draft. It just flowed out of her.[35]

Make time for what restores you, even if that's binge-watching *Law & Order* for three days. A big part of this is to let go of shoulds. Have you set high expectations for your downtime? Fueled by Instagram and reality TV, we put pressure on ourselves to make every moment picture-perfect. But that still makes the moment when we're supposed to be decompressing stressful.

"I don't want quality time," explains comedian Jerry Seinfeld. "I want the garbage time. That's what I like. You just see [your kids] in their room reading a comic book and you get to kind of watch that for a minute, or [having] a bowl of Cheerios at 11 o'clock at night when they're not even supposed to be up. The garbage, that's what I love."[36]

Letting our brains relax makes us healthier—and improves our performance when we reengage with our work or our social lives. One study shows that more than 40 percent of our best creative ideas come when we let our minds wander outside of work time.[37] We've heard this described as the Shower Principle: when you do something comfortable and familiar (like take a long shower), your brain starts to free-associate and comes up with more out-of-the-box solutions. David Goss, who pioneered number theory (a branch of mathematics), said, "All these ideas would come to me via my subconscious. The subconscious mind is a powerful thing. It's almost like the sole reason you do the work is to set the stage for what happens when you step away."[38]

5. What managers and teams can do to prevent and alleviate burnout

MANAGERS: MAKE FINDING BALANCE A COLLECTIVE PRACTICE
WITHIN TEAMS

In our individualistic American culture, we often put the burden of finding balance daily on ourselves. We as individuals *must* carve out time to meditate! In 2015, Amy Bonsall, CEO of nau, a company designed to support flourishing at work, was living and working as a designer in Singapore.[39] She and her team were asked to help a Silicon Valley tech firm reinvent their Singapore workplace. For research, the team traveled to a small island nearby, Pulau Ubin, where people still live in kampong homes (compounds), as they did before Singapore modernized. There is very little individual space, but there are large collective spaces, and everyone has to do his or her share of manual labor. Amy interviewed a Singaporean artist who had left the city to live on the island. Despite the manual labor throughout her day, the artist said she had never been more productive since she had breaks built into her day that allowed for reflection. Amy started to wonder: *Are we stripping out all the things in life that help us regenerate? How can we collectively support each other to find balance?* When Amy moved from Asia back to the United States, she noticed that more Americans were meditating, but often because their watches told them to or because they were trying to get a streak on an app. "We turned this beautiful thing into an individual competitive sport," she said. So Amy started a business to help organizations *collectively* achieve well-being.

In her trainings, Amy starts by explaining that the team is a helpful, and often overlooked, unit to reset together and prevent burnout. On our own, we try to power through eight (or more!) hours with hopes of doing regenerative things like meditation or walks at the end of the day, but we are too exhausted and it's too late. Teams should ask themselves: *How can we incorporate balance as part of our days?*

Amy says it doesn't matter what specifically teams do, as long as it is collective and centers on what matters most to the team—for instance, energy boosting, creativity, and connection. She suggests starting meetings with a short centering practice. Or do a daily fifteen-minute exercise where everyone shares something that is inspiring them. She notes that it will feel weird and counterproductive the first few times. We are used to diving into meeting after meeting, and it feels weak or indulgent to take a break (a common internal refrain is *I would be a better person if I needed no breaks during the day!*). Undoing these habits can be uncomfortable. But we are not machines, and science tells us that we work better if we do take breaks. It helps if we don't do them on our own. There's relief in knowing you're not the only one who is human.

Another suggestion for teams is to dedicate time during the week for no meetings, like meetingless Fridays or Friday afternoons. This is especially true for hybrid or remote work. Research has shown that it's even harder to relax in video calls, exacerbating the already large problem of "meeting fatigue."[40]

LEADERS: TRAIN MANAGERS TO BE SUPPORTIVE AND CREATE REASONABLE WORKLOADS

Dr. Helen Reiss, who studies empathy at Harvard Medical School, says that empathy is a skill that heads off burnout and increases satisfaction at work while also improving general well-being. Being an empathetic leader means fighting against your own biases, listening carefully to your reports, then using any privileges you have (by virtue of your leadership role or other factors) to take action on their behalf. Managers should regularly check in with their teams in a meaningful way. We recommend asking these questions:

- What one thing can I do to better support you? (*Asking "What one thing" solicits more and better responses than "Is there anything I can do?"*)

- What kind of flexibility do you need right now?
- Is anything unclear or blocking your work?
- What was a personal win for you over the past week? What was a challenge?

Perhaps the most important thing you can do as a leader is to create a culture in which workloads are reasonable. According to the World Health Organization, more than 745,000 people died globally in 2016 from overwork. People who work fifty-five or more hours each week have an estimated 35 percent higher risk of a stroke and a 17 percent higher risk of dying from heart disease than people who work thirty-five to forty hours a week.[41] And this was before the pandemic and increased virtual hours! Managers should ensure that employees are not consistently working fifty-five or more hours each week but, ideally, are working forty or fewer hours. Managers should also be open to giving flexible or reduced hours, including paid time off, for those suffering from a mental or physical health problem.

• • •

Even with better management, better teams, and better habits, a stress-free life doesn't exist. There will always be bumps in the road. "Wellness is not a state of being, but a state of action," write the Nagoski sisters.[42] Like many things in life (being able to touch your toes, keeping your fridge stocked, getting your oil changed), avoiding burnout in the modern world requires continual care and practice. Try setting a reminder on your phone or calendar every quarter to ask yourself: Am I slipping into habits again that will lead to burnout?

We'll leave you with a proposal: we often think that, as a reward for working, we get to take vacation, take breaks, and take care of ourselves, but consider the opposite—your health is what allows you to do meaningful work. Your well-being is the foundation for everything else in your life. This is easy to see on an extreme level—if you are having migraines so bad that you can only lie in bed and close your eyes, it's impossible to work—but it is also true on an everyday scale. If you have overworked yourself one day, you need to get back in balance.

PICK YOUR PATH

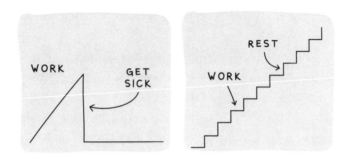

MOLLIE: *I wish I could tell you there was a nice, neat wrap-up to my story, but I want you to know that's not true. When I got over my cold and flu, I went to San Francisco for our book launch, and then later I went to London. Our book did not suffer from it. At IDEO, I asked to be put on projects that didn't require travel at work. So, in some ways, I was taking better care of myself.*

But while I addressed the immediate issue, my illness led to a series of chronic health problems I'm still recovering from (see chapter 6). In fact, much of the process of "writing" this book for me was actually dictating, because tendon issues in my hands and elbows still make it painful to type. At one point during the worst of it, my husband had to tie my shoes for me, prepare every meal, and drive me everywhere I needed to go. (I'm incredibly grateful for his endless patience and good humor.) And yet I still kept pushing myself, trying to avoid coming to terms with my complete emotional and physical burnout.

For me, asking for changes at work and cutting back on travel was only part of the solution. The bigger piece involved lots of self work and restructuring most of my life over the course of a year. What would it take to prevent burnout in the future? First, my husband and I made the tough decision to move from New York to Los Angeles, where the pace of life was a bit slower and more conducive to my healing. It took me six months to stop regretting this decision and to let go of the crazy-yet-addicting life I'd been living. (As my therapist said to me, "New York is a hell of a drug.") Next, I decided to take a few months off from book events (Liz generously did them solo).

Once the flurry of my life had slowed a bit, I realized I had tuned out the needs of my mind, soul, and body for the past few years. I had forgotten that Mollie needed Mollie time. (Joey Soloway's bumper sticker to the contrary, I realized downtime had never made me anxious as a child—quite the opposite!)

I continued work with my therapist, slowly convincing myself that I was worthy of love and self-love even if I didn't work at a rock star consulting firm, exercise every day, stay in good contact with every friend I had, answer emails within twenty-four hours, keep my house totally clean, have a baby when all my friends were having babies, and, of course, post about it all on social media.

I decided to take some time off and then find a job where my work was more self-directed and longer-term. I started saying no to more things than I was saying yes to. I even watched TV on some weekend afternoons (egad!!).

While I sometimes have nostalgia for my previous turbo life in New York, I also know that leaving it was necessary. As Pema Chödrön writes, "Things falling apart is a kind of testing and also a kind of healing." But the healing comes only if we are willing to bear witness to what needs to change and then get uncomfortable by taking on that change. "Most of us do not take these situations as teachings. We automatically hate them. We run like crazy," Chödrön writes.[43] Instead, we have to feel the exhaustion and the emotions that follow. Burnout is your body and soul forcing you to pay attention to them. Healing from burnout involves learning what your own innate pace of life is and then inhabiting that pace.

This isn't easy. I am still very much trying to figure it out. When starting to write this book, I slipped back into my old habit of putting pressure on myself. I hate having deadlines loom over me, so my tendency is to get things done well before the deadline (I was a do-my-homework-on-Friday-night kid). Overworking is, in a way, an anxiety-management technique. There will always be something hanging over me, so instead I am learning to live with the incomplete.

TAKEAWAYS

- Burnout is not obvious: watch out for the early warning signs
- Take care of yourself before you're completely fried
- Figure out whether you're overextended, disengaged, or feeling ineffective
- If you're overextended, get comfortable living at 80 percent and say no more often
- If you're disengaged, seek connection and craft a more meaningful schedule
- If you feel ineffective, find ways to achieve clear wins and realign your life with your values
- If you feel all three, detach your worth from your work and embrace "garbage time"
- Managers and leaders: make balance a collective goal, offer emotional support, and avoid overworking your teams
- Remember that your health is what allows you to do meaningful work

CHAPTER 5

Perfectionism

Perfectionism doesn't make you feel perfect;
it makes you feel inadequate.

LIZ: *For most of my life, I thought I had to be perfect to be loved.*

A few months into dating Maxim (now my husband), I got horrible food poisoning. When I called to cancel our dinner plans, Maxim asked if he could come by with chicken broth and ginger ale. Touched, I took him up on his offer. But the moment I hung up, panic gripped me. In my sweaty sickness, I had forgotten: my apartment was in a state of disarray.

I shot out of bed and started frantically cleaning the house. I snatched clothes off the floor, cleared a few half-empty mugs from the coffee table, and arranged the pillows on the couch. Then I sprinted to the bathroom and threw up.

Looking back, OMG.

At the time, I didn't see anything wrong with my obsessive drive to come across as perfect; this was just what it took to be worthy of someone's affection. The curated version of me that never had a hair or throw pillow out of place, the one Maxim was falling in love with, was far better than the real me.

But when Maxim asked me to move in with him several months later, my façade was in serious danger of crumbling. If we spent all our time together, Maxim would quickly uncover the messy, emotional wreck that I had worked so hard to hide.

Here were the problems: My favorite cozy bedtime pants were graying men's long underwear with a hole in the butt. After particularly hard workdays, I liked to stand in the kitchen, pour soy sauce on popcorn until it was soggy, and then eat it with a spoon. Sometimes at night, I was seized with existential angst and would have to pace the perimeter of my apartment like a trapped animal until I wore myself out. Maxim didn't know about any of that.

Each day, I got more anxious about cohabitation. "What's wrong?" he would ask me. The right words always floated just beyond my reach. "I'm fine," I'd reply, clenching my jaw. It felt as if an invisible fist was tightly squeezing my chest from the inside. Maxim was going to see me for the imperfect, undatable person I was. And then he would leave me. So the conversation looped back around, no resolution in sight. "But I can tell something is wrong," Maxim countered.

One day, he finally told me, "I want to help you, and you're obviously upset, but you're not letting me in. If you can't figure out a way to open up, I don't know if we can make this work."

My need to come across as perfect was driving Maxim away. Something needed to change.

• • •

In 2005, psychologists Gordon Flett and Paul Hewitt set out to determine how perfectionism affects performance.[1] Their discovery? It makes a big difference, but not in the way you might expect.

Looking at professional athletes, they found that people who displayed more perfectionist tendencies became overly concerned with their mistakes. Their fear of failure undermined their potential and made them do *worse* compared with their peers.[2]

Generally speaking, perfectionism is an unrealistic drive to be flawless, combined with intense negative self-talk. It's one thing to strive for 100 percent, get a 94 percent, and feel good about what you've learned. It's another, poisonous thing to beat yourself up for a 99 percent.

Over the past thirty years, the desire to be perfect has shot up by nearly 33 percent in the Western world.[3] Responses from nearly fifty thousand US, Ca-

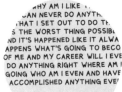

nadian, and British college students who completed a perfectionism question-naire between 1989 and 2016 show that we've become far more likely to be hard on ourselves and to want to present a spotless image.[4]

Researchers point to two main catalysts behind this dramatic uptick: the internet and our free-market, meritocratic system.[5] We're guessing you're familiar with how bad social media platforms like Instagram, LinkedIn, and TikTok can make us feel about ourselves. Since we covered this in chapter 2, here we're going to focus more on the second driver.

Sharing and civic responsibility are increasingly being replaced with self-interest and competition.[6] We're ranked and sorted through a dizzying array of metrics: test scores, performance assessments, job titles, our social media presences, our hobbies-forced-to-become-résumé-boosters—the list goes on. And when you internalize the edicts of the free market—that your worth is a direct product of your effort—you start to believe that if you're not as well off as someone else, you're lazy and have personally failed in some deep, fundamental way. "You didn't come onto this earth as a perfectionist or control freak. You weren't born a person of cringe and contraction," writes author Anne Lamott in *Stitches: A Handbook on Meaning, Hope and Repair*. "You learned contraction to survive."[7]

Being in a historically underrepresented group can add to the pressure to be seen as perfect. Women are more likely to experience perfectionism than men. And research shows that racial discrimination is also linked with perfectionist tendencies—and depression.[8] "Growing up, I was told that I need to work twice as hard as my white peers," Jade, a Black marketing manager, told us. "Now I feel this constant hum of anxiety to prove that I deserved my promotion."[9]

How can you move forward in light of these forces? In this chapter, we'll prove that many beliefs we hold about perfectionism are far from perfect. While you can't escape systemic forces, you can begin to prioritize your mental well-being and happiness. We'll pinpoint the mind-sets that keep you stuck, and we'll give you a guide for moving forward with a healthier worldview. Finally, we'll equip you with tools for when perfectionism tries to pull you back into its clutches.

PERFECTIONISM

FEEL LIKE I
COULD BE
DOING MORE

DO MORE

Before we get started, it's worth being clear: Moving past the pitfalls of perfectionism is not about hitting certain goals. (We know. As two reformed perfectionists, we love goals, too.) It's about recovering from it through internal acceptance and self-compassion.

MYTHS ABOUT PERFECTIONISM

Myth #1: Perfectionism always presents in color-coded folders and elaborate daily routines

It's easy to assume that perfectionists appear, well, perfect. We tend to equate perfectionism with type-A traits, like being very organized, ambitious, and put together. But perfectionism is driven by low self-esteem and centers on avoiding failure.

Many people who have perfectionist tendencies don't identify as perfectionists because they have such high standards for themselves that they think they are closer to being failures than to being perfect. But there's no one-size-fits-all version of perfectionism. Here are some clues that you've tied your worth too closely to meeting an unrealistic ideal:

- You never feel good about what you've done. You obsess, sometimes to the point where you miss important deadlines or regret trying at all.
- You need a permission slip to see yourself as knowledgeable or worthy. You keep thinking you'll have something to contribute once you hit a specific milestone or get that certification or degree, but until then, you know nothing.
- You're unable to shut off. When you try to step away from a project, you can't stop creating mental checklists.
- You're a people pleaser. Without validation from those around you, you feel worthless and ruminate about what you might have done wrong. Your self-confidence (and sense of satisfaction) is, as clinical psychologist Michael Brustein puts it, "a gas tank with a hole in it."[10]
- You're so tired, but the only way you can imagine digging yourself out of your exhaustion is to do more.
- You devalue your accomplishments. If your friend says she's impressed

by you, you think she's saying that only because she knows nothing about your industry.

If these bullet points resonate with you, you're not alone. When reader Nataly and her husband moved from Southern California to Oregon, she saw a chance for a fresh start. She had just taken up running, stopped smoking, and landed a great new job, and she was excited about how healthy and fabulous her new life was going to be.

But moving away from her friends was harder than she'd anticipated, and the stress of starting the new job left her feeling anxious and inadequate. Nataly started to get frustrated that her life wasn't going as swimmingly as she had hoped it would. To try to wrest back some control, she went on a keto diet and began tracking her macros. "I became kind of an asshole," she recalled. "I'm so embarrassed to think back on conversations I had about my diet during that time, especially with friends who are heavier than me."

Nataly didn't recognize what she was doing as perfectionism until her therapist pointed it out.* "I just felt like I was finally on the path to becoming the person I was supposed to be, and if I could just push myself a little harder, I would get there."[11]

Perfectionism is often context-specific. You might feel pressure to present perfectly in social situations, or you might have job-based perfectionism. In short, even if your house is messy or you haven't been promoted in the last six months, you still might be struggling with perfectionist tendencies.

In fact, perfectionism often manifests as procrastination. Liz's friend Jay loves photography but refuses to share his photos until he's 100 percent happy with his edits. He'll take a picture of a casual hike in March and send it to his friends in April—two years later. Once, when Liz was visiting him, she found him at his

---

*Perfectionism and a need for control can often manifest as disordered eating. If you are experiencing disordered eating, visit nationaleatingdisorders.org to find support and resources.

desk, trying to get a smiling man's tooth to be the perfect shade of white. Liz took a shower, had breakfast, answered some emails, walked around the block, and when she came back, Jay was still zoomed in on that one tooth.

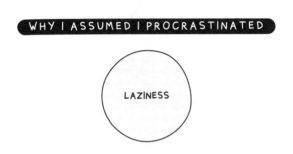

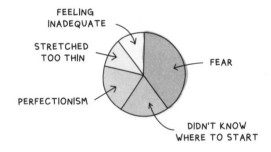

Myth #2: Perfectionists get things done

You might think, "It would be great if my surgeon, financial adviser, or reporter were a perfectionist!"

"Not quite," psychologist Thomas S. Greenspon, author of *Moving Past Perfect*, told us. "Across jobs, the most successful people are less likely to be perfectionists. That's because the anxiety about making mistakes gets in your way."[12]

"Perfectionism can be paralyzing," confirms reader and physician Dr. Kara

Pepper. "I've seen doctors spend longer in surgery or overthink a diagnosis due to self-doubt."[13]

By obsessing too much over getting it exactly right, we undermine our ability to succeed. When high achievers mess up, they see it as a learning experience, course-correct, and move on. Perfectionists get stuck, revisiting even the smallest mistake over and over and making themselves feel terrible about even trying at all. This is called the *perfection paradox*: we're so afraid of failing that we have a hard time doing.[14]

People who feel the need to be perfect tend to be all-or-nothing thinkers. Either you're the best at something or it was a waste of time; either you hit your goal or you didn't make any progress at all. Perfectionists often give up when even the smallest thing goes wrong.

In an experiment, researchers gave perfectionists and nonperfectionists specific goals. They also rigged the test so that everyone was doomed to fail. Guess which group quickly gave up? The perfectionists felt ashamed and tapped out early, while the not-so-perfect group kept plugging away, learning and having fun.[15]

The key to success is practice, which involves errors, failure, and asking questions. It's far better to share an early draft and get feedback than to spend weeks "perfecting" it in isolation only to realize it's not really what your boss had in mind.

Some of us are so afraid of failure that we never try. Have you ever read the requirements for a job, realized that you have seven years of experience but the company is asking for eight to ten, and then immediately disqualified yourself? That's the cost of perfectionism.

Myth #3: You have to be perfect to be valued

The next time you start to feel frantic, try to pinpoint what you're afraid of. Chances are beneath that fear of not meeting a deadline, missing your child's soccer game, or falling short of your standards as a partner is a deep fear of not being worthy, of not being loved as you are.

Perfectionists tend to feel like they're not full people. It's fine for *others* to make mistakes, because those individuals are worthy. "But not me," perfectionists think. "I need to prove I'm deserving of love."

While some of our tendencies are due to genetics, perfectionism is often a response to trauma. Children who have to mediate or manage their parents' emotions are especially likely to grow into perfectionist adults. Early on, they learn that their environments aren't stable or safe unless they step in to help.

Reader Katja's father mentally and physically abused her as a child. Growing up, Katja did whatever she could to please him, hoping that it would spare her from his cruelty. "I spent snow days cleaning out the fridge or organizing and alphabetizing the spice rack," she told us.

Katja carried her perfectionist beliefs into adulthood: even when she was happily married, she frequently stayed up late to make sure her kitchen counter didn't have a speck of dirt on it. Then one day, she came across the quote "Perfectionism is a form of self-abuse." She was floored. "That quote changed my life," Katja told us. "I'd worked so hard to rid my life of abusive relationships, and here I was abusing myself."[16]

Even if you grew up in a loving and supportive environment, you still may have received messages that focused on the value of achievement. Maybe your parents took you out for ice cream when you got a good grade or won a soccer game but said nothing when you didn't excel or your team lost. Over time, you internalized the idea that you deserve love only when you've done something well.[17]

Perfectionism gives us a sense of control, which can offer short-term emotional relief. We tell ourselves that if we do everything right, we can avoid rejection and abuse. Psychologists refer to this as *magical thinking*, when we believe that one thing causes another when there isn't an obvious link.

But, of course, perfect is impossible. And no matter what you do in life, bad things might still happen.

Shame and guilt

We feel shame when we attribute a flaw to ourselves rather than to our behavior. Guilt, on the other hand, is when we're upset because of a specific action. Say you forget to respond to a friend's email. Shame is when you tell yourself, "I'm a bad person." Guilt is "I did a bad thing."

Shame makes us withdraw. We believe that *we* are the thing that is wrong and don't want to burden people with our presence. When we feel guilt, we think we *did* something wrong, which makes it easier to map out ways to make things right. In fact, research shows that when we experience guilt, we pay more attention to words like *help* and *apologize* than we normally would.[18]

A powerful way to move through shame is to open up to people you trust. "If we can share our story with someone who responds with empathy and understanding, shame can't survive," explains author Brené Brown.[19] By revealing what you've been struggling to keep hidden away, you move from thinking, "I can never share this, and I am a bad person," to "I'm not the only one—in fact, my friend did or felt something similar. She is not a bad person, so I must not be either."

A participant in one of our workshops shared with us how helpful online support communities can be as a space for sharing shame. They told us, "Online communities can be helpful for people who have been victims of domestic violence or have medical conditions. It's easier to share your story with people who have opted in."

Studies show that another way to reduce shame is to try to turn it into guilt. When you think, "I'm a horrible person because I forgot to respond to the email," refocus on a specific behavior by telling yourself, "I forgot, and I feel bad about it." Then see if you can apologize or correct your mistake. Remember: you are not a fundamentally flawed person. Sure, there may be things you need to work on, but you *can* work on them.

Also see "Resources on shame and guilt" on page 235.

. . .

LIZ: *At Maxim's gentle urging, I started seeing a therapist to help me get out of my own way.*

During one of our first sessions, my therapist asked me to describe an experience I enjoyed with a pet. An image of Sophie, a grumpy Persian fluff ball, immediately popped into my head.

A few months earlier, we had been house-sitting for Maxim's aunt and uncle, and part of the job was to take care of Sophie. She was

seventeen (that is, old) and breathed in raspy little snorts. I'd be work-
ing on the couch, and after a while, she'd slowly amble up and plop
down next to me. She was the opposite of a doting puppy: her face was
always squished into a dour scowl, and her exhale-snorts made her
seem even more put off by the world around her. But I loved having
her furry little body next to mine.

"Sophie made you happy," my therapist pointed out. "Just by sitting
next to you. She wasn't cracking jokes or impressing you with counter-
intuitive facts. She was just there, existing, and that was enough."

Over the next few weeks, my therapist helped me gather the cour-
age to open up more. He outlined slow, measured steps I could take to
become more vulnerable around Maxim, whom I trusted to be loving
and supportive. I made a soggy bowl of soy sauce popcorn and ate it in
front of him. When I had a panic attack, I told Maxim, "I'm starting
to get really anxious," and had him hug me.

When I thought about the times I'd felt closest to loved ones, it was
always when they opened up and shared their anxieties or weaknesses.
I realized that by trying to present myself as superhuman, I was pre-
venting them from experiencing that same closeness with me.

Out of everything my therapist and I talked about, the Sophie
story sticks with me the most. "She was just there, existing, and that
was enough." I always thought I needed to be amazing, funny, and
positive to be loved and to make someone else happy. But often, all we
need to do is be there.

HOW TO WORK THROUGH IT

While perfectionism can show up in many small, private ways, it tends to present along similar lines of all-or-nothing thinking: "If I stumble over my words just once during my presentation at the next company all-hands meeting, I will never be seen as a leader," or "If my friends see that my living room is messy, they'll judge me and won't like me anymore."

In this section, we'll help you untangle yourself from these kinds of statements and start to embrace a more self-compassionate, realistic outlook.

And remember: if you slip up here and there on the path to recovery, that's okay. As with all things in life, it won't be a perfect process.

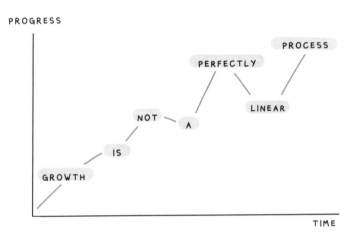

1. Scrap the idea that perfectionism serves you

As the Zen proverb goes, "Let go or get dragged."

People with perfectionist tendencies don't realize that their success happens *in spite of* their drive for flawlessness, not because of it. "What I often say to my patients," psychologist Thomas S. Greenspon told us, "is that if I could wave a magic wand and get rid of your perfectionism, you'd be *more* successful. Your success is due to your energy, your talent, your commitment, and none of those things would go away."[20]

One of the most destructive aspects of perfectionism is that it prevents us from being kind to ourselves. We fear that if we relax, we'll become complacent and indulgent. Psychologist Jessica Pryor has observed that many of her perfectionist clients are afraid she'll "turn them into some degenerate couch potato and teach them to be okay with it."[21]

But cutting ourselves some slack makes us more likely to improve—and less likely to give up. In one experiment, when participants journaled about why they might benefit from a little self-compassion, they were far more likely to treat themselves with kindness over the following week. As a result, they also felt and performed better.[22]

WE THINK OF FAILURE AND SUCCESS AS OPPOSITES

WHEN IN REALITY FAILURE IS PART OF SUCCESS

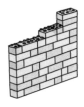

Our need to be perfect can also prevent us from forming deeper connections. Reader Kimberly used to agonize so much over crafting texts and emails that she sometimes never replied at all, which ultimately made her life *more* rather than *less* difficult. While the goal of perfectionism is to be liked, "instead, it pushes people away—that's the neurotic paradox," explains psychologist Paul Hewitt.[23]

And finally, perfectionism tends to undermine your leadership abilities. Researchers identified three types of managers:

- The **good enough manager**, who sets clear goals but then lets employees figure out how to get there
- The **not good enough manager**, who is all over the place or rarely checks in
- The **uber manager**, who is a perfectionist with rigid standards for how every step of the process should be completed

When asked to choose which one they'd like to work for, most people chose the "good enough manager."[24] If you've ever worked for a micromanager, that finding shouldn't come as a surprise. Having someone oversee and nitpick every move you make can be a powerful motivator—to find another job.

So be honest about how much your perfectionism is costing you. Ask yourself:

- How is it impacting my mental health?
- How is it affecting my relationships?
- How might it be holding me back at work?

2. Explore where you learned that you were not good enough

If you're a perfectionist, chances are at some point you learned that anything less than extraordinary meant pain or rejection. Reader Meg's parents set high academic and professional standards for her. When she got a B, her parents stopped speaking to her for weeks. Over time, Meg internalized these messages and started to berate herself so much for making even a small mistake that it often left her unable to move forward.[25] In medical school, Kara, the physician we quoted earlier, was conditioned to believe that anything less than perfect was dishonorable and lazy. Even when she was suffering from severe gastroenteritis, she still came in to work, where she completed her hospital rounds attached to an IV pole.[26]

Reaching what we've come to see as "perfect" does provide us emotional relief—but only for a moment. In the long run, perfectionism hurts us far more than it helps. Meg is now estranged from her parents and still gets anxious if people come into her house when it's not spotless. And Kara nearly left medicine due to burnout.

To begin charting a better course for yourself, write out your perfectionist thoughts and then reflect on these prompts:

- Where did I learn to set this expectation for myself?
- What is my perfectionism trying to protect me from?
- If I meet this expectation, will I actually be protected from what I fear?
- What do I wish I could say to my younger self?

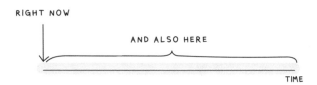

Recognizing the impact these stories have on us can make it easier to push back against them. As an immigrant and a woman of color, reader Yanelle used to feel constant pressure to prove she deserved her job. "There are people out there who don't think I'm worthy of the things I have achieved," she told us. Over time, she began to prioritize her own happiness over working tirelessly, and spent more time with a group of friends with whom she felt she could be herself. "I literally said 'Fuck it' and decided that I need to live my life on my own terms."[27]

3. Untangle yourself from perfectionist self-narratives

Once you've identified the stories and expectations you've internalized, the next step is to move away from them. We've found these three questions to be helpful:

- Who am I without labels or roles?
- How would a friend describe me?
- What do I want or need, free of expectations?

The goal of the first two prompts is to help you identify what makes you worthy and lovable just for being you—separate from your performance, appearance, or status. Try to avoid using descriptors that fall into these buckets:

1. How well you do (e.g., "successful" or "high earner")
2. What you look like (e.g., "pretty" or "muscular")
3. What people think of you (e.g., "a role model" or "powerful")

In other words, if you couldn't say that you were a top student or a mom or the child of immigrants, how would you portray yourself? What do your friends love about you? (Hint: We're guessing they wouldn't start off by gushing over your ability to get to inbox zero.) If you're having trouble getting started, here are some examples we heard from readers: *I'm funny and generous. I'm principled. I'm open-minded instead of judgmental. I try to understand other perspectives. I'm a good listener. I love to learn. I'm not afraid of challenges. I'm sincere. I'm goofy.*

And the third question: Who would you be if you didn't feel pressure to follow someone else's rules? Liz's immigrant parents encouraged her, when she was growing up, to become a neurosurgeon, a wealth manager, or a corporate lawyer. But after two years of staring at a Bloomberg terminal until 1 A.M. as a consultant, she burned out. For weeks, she dreaded telling her parents that she was going to quit. When she finally called them, she was surprised that they supported her decision. Her parents had never been ill-intentioned: they wanted what was good for Liz (a stable, lucrative career), but that wasn't what ended up being *best* for her (a career that involved a bit more risk but was personally meaningful).

Because of her physical disability, reader Elizabeth's colleagues often

perceived her as "superhuman," a somewhat suffocating label. For years, she felt compelled to portray a "perpetually cheerful disabled person" who never complained and could solve all her problems by herself. It took time, and a new job, for Elizabeth to realize that she could ask for help and still be perceived as competent.[28]

4. Replace "avoidance goals" with "approach goals"

If your goal is to not fail, you'll never feel that good. "Not failing" isn't a fulfilling milestone or reason to get excited.

To break the cycle, start setting what psychologists call *approach goals* (achieving a positive) instead of *avoidance goals* (preventing a negative). For example, if you're going to give a presentation at work, say to yourself, "I want to impress people with my compelling storytelling" (approach goal) rather than "I want to avoid looking like I don't know what I'm doing" (avoidance goal).

Avoiding failure can certainly be motivating (Liz studied hard in high school to avoid disappointing her parents), but it comes with a lot of stress and pressure. And every time you think about your goal, you feel bad. "Don't disappoint Mom and Dad!" isn't the most uplifting phrase to have banging around your brain for years. An approach goal, on the other hand, is motivating *and* exciting, because there's something to really celebrate if you accomplish it. For high school Liz, that might have been "Get into your dream college in California."

The key is to start small, and in a loving and supportive environment. To heal from perfectionism, therapist Rebecca Newkirk told us, you need your "body and brain to experience itself as safe inside a situation that might activate a trauma response." And be wary of turning to your family or the people you grew up with for support in your recovery process. "Often you're looking for them to meet a need that they created," says Rebecca. "So even if you love each other, they're probably not the best people to be stretching yourself with, at least initially."[29]

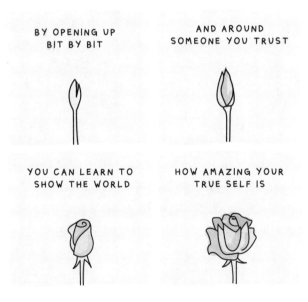

BY OPENING UP
BIT BY BIT

AND AROUND
SOMEONE YOU TRUST

YOU CAN LEARN TO
SHOW THE WORLD

HOW AMAZING YOUR
TRUE SELF IS

As they settled into their new living arrangement, Liz knew she could trust Maxim, so instead of setting avoidance goals, like "act in a way that prevents

Maxim from seeing me as weak and needy," she set herself tiny approach goals, like "The next time I feel gloomy, I'll tell Maxim and give him the opportunity to comfort me." After she opened up in small ways, she'd check in with how it felt. Over time, she got more and more comfortable sharing her feelings, because she had more and more proof that even in her darker moments, her support system would still be there. She taught herself that she didn't need to be perfect to be loved.

5. Recognize when good enough is good enough

There comes a point when continuing to work on something either won't make a big difference or, by obsessing so much, you will start to actively hurt yourself.

Dave, a leader at the sports website *Bleacher Report*, encourages his teams (and himself) to share their work when they think it's 80 percent there. "A project can often be deemed complete before its perfectionist creator feels it's really done," he told us. "In fact, other people may not know the difference between 80 percent finished and 100 percent finished." In his experience, it's also easier to iterate on an 80 percent project than on something you consider 100 percent.[30]

Stopping when you've hit "good enough" requires you to let go of your all-or-nothing mind-set. A lot of things that are worth doing at 100 percent are still worth doing at 20 percent. Even if you don't run five miles, a one-mile run is better than nothing. Consultant Becky keeps a Post-it note near her desk that says, "B+ work can change the world, but work that doesn't get done helps no one."[31]

Getting comfortable with good enough requires practice and might feel extremely bad in the moment. To see if she could help staff members overcome their perfectionist tendencies, Alice Provost, a counselor at the University of California, Davis, asked them to slack off a bit. She encouraged them to get to the office at 9 A.M. and head home no later than 5 P.M., take their entire lunch break, and leave their desks a bit messy. In the moment, the staff members felt horrible. But on reflection, they recognized that "the things they [had been] so worried about weren't that crucial."[32]

PERFECTIONIST LIGHT SWITCHES

Embracing "good enough" can also help you combat procrastination. Remind yourself that we learn by doing. If you want to become good at something, the fastest way to get there is to practice. Here are three questions to help you break free of procrastination:

1. How will I feel in the long run if I don't try?
2. What's the smallest first step I could take?
3. If I could do one thing to achieve my goal, what would it be?[33]

We also heard from many readers that they find it useful to say to themselves, "I'm going to do this for five minutes, and then I can quit."

6. Get rid of *always* and *never*

These words are usually signs of perfectionist, all-or-nothing tendencies. "Great employees always turn everything in on time." "Good moms never get frustrated with their kids."

Harvard psychologist Dr. Ellen Langer found that our words have a big impact on our behavior.[34] In an experiment, people who made a mistake with a pencil were given access to several objects, including a rubber band. Of those who were told, "This is a rubber band," only 3 percent realized it could also function as an eraser. But in the group that was told, "This *could* be a rubber band," almost half figured out that they could use it to erase their error.

The next time you catch yourself thinking the word *always* or *never*, reframe the situation. Say you're too exhausted after work to join your friends for dinner. Instead of thinking, "I always let people down," tell yourself, "I'm skipping one event to take care of myself." You can also remind yourself of all the times you *did* show up.

In her first few weeks as an intern, reader Bethanny had trouble sleeping, because she was so concerned about her performance at work. "I thought that interns could never make mistakes," she told us, "and should always be the last ones in the office." Then Bethanny's therapist asked her if her manager had set those expectations. "It dawned on me that no one was telling me I wasn't good enough except me," Bethanny recalled. She started to relax at work—she asked more questions and left the office a bit earlier in the evening—and still got a job offer at the end of the summer.[35]

WHEN YOU FIND YOURSELF THINKING:

I'M A FAILURE

REFRAME AND KEEP GOING:

THAT WAS A FAILED ATTEMPT

No one is perfect. Even the most successful people overlook emails, get pimples, and have off days. So right now, take a moment to identify one lofty, possibly subconscious expectation you've made for yourself recently. Then let it go.

7. Name your inner perfectionist, and find a nonperfectionist role model

To put some psychological distance between you and your inner critic, try giving it a name. For example, author Amber Rae refers to her inner perfectionist as Grace. When she feels compelled to run herself ragged, she tells herself, "Oh, that's Grace."[36] And instead of silencing Grace, Amber asks her, "What are you afraid of? What do you need to feel safe? How can we work together?" These questions also allow Amber to alchemize Grace from a guard into a guide. "Generally, Grace needs a dose of reassurance," Amber told us. "And when I can help her feel safer and less afraid, I'm able to channel Grace's gifts: she's very detailed, she has an exacting eye, she has impeccable taste."

Executive coach Melody Wilding recommends choosing a silly name or a character from a movie or a book (Melody calls her own inner perfectionist Bozo). "I once had a client who called his Darth Vader," she writes. "He purchased a small Darth Vader action figure for his desk, which reminded him to keep the critical voice in check."[37]

You can also identify people you admire who do not have perfectionist tendencies. Perhaps you even admire them more because they have a sense of "the big picture." Mollie was recently feeling guilty about not keeping in better touch with friends by text and phone. So she reached out to a friend, and they played phone tag. Mollie then texted her to find a time, and her friend responded, "Hi love, sorry for being flaky. Truth be told, I'm going through IVF right now so my days have been hit and miss. I get a break in a few weeks, so maybe we can chat then." Mollie loved this message, partly because she could empathize with her friend's guilt and overwhelm, and partly because she admired her friend's courage.

. . .

LIZ: *It's still hard for me to really open up to people. And when I do show vulnerability, I always feel compelled to tie it up neatly with a joke or a "but I'm actually totally fine." In fact, while writing this book, Mollie pointed out that this tendency was showing up in my stories for each chapter: "I was extremely anxious for three months, but I learned how to cope, and presto-pasta, everything is smooth sailing."*

The truth: my perfectionism still pops up now and then. Sometimes, Maxim has to ask me more than once before I'll finally admit that I'm feeling glum. But I've gotten a lot better. Now I know that my old emotional convictions were based on inaccurate assumptions (that Maxim would leave me if I were anything less than perfect), so it's easier (mostly) for me to unhook myself from them and just tell him, "I'm really stressed today and annoyed by the way you're slurping your coffee so loudly." (See? Still have to end on a joke.)

TAKEAWAYS

- You can have perfectionist tendencies even if you feel far from perfect
- Scrap the idea that perfectionism serves you
- Explore where you learned that you need to be perfect to be valued
- Poke holes in your perfectionist self-talk
- Replace avoidance goals with approach goals
- Recognize when good enough is good enough
- Move away from all-or-nothing thinking, and avoid the words *always* and *never*
- Name your inner perfectionist, and seek an imperfect role model

CHAPTER 6

Despair

A note and trigger warning: This chapter contains descriptions of suicidal thoughts. We are not licensed therapists, and the advice we give worked for Mollie but may not work for you. This chapter is not intended to be a substitute for getting help. If you are experiencing suicidal thoughts, please call the National Suicide Prevention Lifeline at 800-273-8255 or see "Resources on suicide" on page 236. You can also reach out to a friend or relative you trust. Even if you don't want to talk, just having someone present (in person or on the phone) can keep you from harming yourself.

Life begins on the other side of despair.

Jean-Paul Sartre

MOLLIE: *Eight months after our first book came out and two months after my thirty-second birthday, I stopped wanting to be alive.*

This is not an easy story for me to share. I am a private person, and it's hard for me to imagine my extended family knowing all of this, let alone the public. But because there is such stigma around these feelings, I think it's important to share.

I had no history of depression or mental illness. I was usually an upbeat person, and I had a good job and a stable marriage. My colleagues described me as unflappable. My friends jokingly called me "The President," because I brought our group together and organized reunions and surprise birthday gifts. My husband described me as incredibly calm and even-keeled.

But all those traits disappeared. I had been dealing with chronic foot pain for months, and it was so bad I couldn't walk for more than ten minutes or stand for more than five minutes without pain. My doctors could offer only symptomatic relief, and when that didn't work, they believed the pain was in my head. Desperate, I agreed to let a doctor do an experimental blood plasma injection, which made the pain worse. My husband, Chris, and I had just moved to LA, and I had no friends. I was working from home and was extremely isolated. We were ready to start trying for a kid, but in the previous three months, my period had gone away because of stress (which can happen when your body produces too much of the stress hormone cortisol), making it impossible to get pregnant. I could no longer use my main coping mechanisms for anxiety, walking and running. I hadn't been sleeping for weeks. I couldn't see a way that any of this would get better. I knew the pain wasn't in my head, but how could I get the help I needed if doctors didn't believe me? How would my period come back if I was still so stressed about my pain? How would I find a new job when I was so depressed I could barely do the work I had?

My dreams for a life worth living were replaced with the desire to jump in front of a train. On a flight from LA to San Francisco (I was commuting twice a month for work), I picked out a train number and location and put it in the Notes app on my phone. I wrote a goodbye note to my family. My plan was to leave the note in my hotel room and then take a Lyft to the BART station. When I got to the hotel from the airport, I sat down at the desk and reread my goodbye note. I started shaking. I couldn't make myself call a car. I left the hotel and walked along the Embarcadero. It was unseasonably warm for October, and San Francisco was heady with it. People ran and strolled by, oblivious of me. I walked in physical and mental pain, tears streaming down my face. I went back to the hotel, lay on the bed, and cried myself to sleep with my clothes on.

This is despair.

* * *

*D*espair is not a word people frequently use to describe their emotional state. Despair wasn't even clinically defined with a scaled set of criteria until 2020.[1] Researchers now point to seven indicators of this emotion:

* Feeling hopeless
* Having low self-esteem
* Feeling unloved
* Worrying frequently
* Loneliness

. Helplessness

. Feeling sorry for oneself[2]

Some of these indicators overlap with diagnostic criteria for major depression or generalized anxiety disorder. But the last three (loneliness, helplessness, and feeling sorry for oneself) are not symptoms of any other specific psychiatric disorder.[3] In other words, despair involves feeling depressed and anxious, but piling on feeling hopeless, lonely, unloved, helpless, and sorry for yourself pushes you into the intensity of despair. If Mollie had looked at this list, she would have checked off all seven indicators.

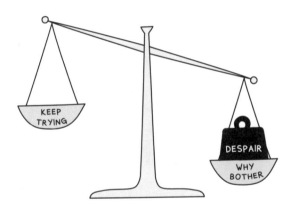

Despair is on the rise in the United States, as are deaths from despair (deaths from suicide, alcohol, or drug use). Deaths of despair are one of the primary reasons that life expectancy here has decreased since 2016. Researchers found that symptoms of despair increased across all demographics as people entered their thirties.[4] The researchers attribute this increase in despair to a combination of the thirties being a stressful phase of life and a society with worsening job options and fewer social connections.

Your version of despair might not be as dangerous and potentially life-threatening as Mollie's was. You might feel stuck in a seemingly hopeless job, relationship, or other situation. You might feel isolated and alone. Maybe you're not dealing with despair yourself, but you have a loved one who is struggling. Or maybe you are where Mollie was, or worse, in which case we strongly urge you to talk to a mental health professional (it made a world of difference for Mollie) or **call the National Suicide Prevention Lifeline at 800-273-8255**. For more on how to find mental health support, see "Resources on suicide" on page 236. You can also reach out to a friend or relative you trust. Even if you don't want to talk, just having someone present (in person or on the phone) can keep you from harming yourself.

Regardless of what despair looks like for you, we know from personal experience and the research that it's best to seek help right away. There are ways to move through despair, but they should always go hand in hand with support from a professional, as it is very hard to work through this emotion on your own. Unfortunately, there is no secret life hack that will magically rid you of despair—and it takes time to go away. Some of the advice we'll give in this chapter is just about how to make it through a single dark moment.

But first, we want to help you unlearn three tales we're often told about despair.

MYTHS ABOUT DESPAIR

Myth #1: Just focus on something else and you'll be fine

The most dangerous myth is that suffering can be remedied by the right distraction, a sunny pep talk, or a reminder to look on the bright side. Asking people to ignore their despair is as ineffective, harmful, and cruel as telling them to get over a loved one dying or to disregard the throbbing pain of a broken bone.

Recovery starts by taking despair seriously. When you admit you're going through a hard time, you're not wallowing or displaying weakness. You're taking the first step toward being heard (sometimes even just by yourself) and finding ways to not feel so totally alone.

Many people are afraid to name and address their own despair, because there is shame around it and fear of being labeled "crazy" or "dangerous." (For a while before she told her husband or therapist about her suicidal thoughts, Mollie was worried that opening up to them would land her immediately in a psych ward.) Additionally, many people are afraid of not knowing what to say when a loved one is in despair. But research shows that having open, nonjudgmental conversations in which family or friends can voice those fears, tell the person they care about them, and leave space for them to share their honest state of mind makes it less likely they'll act on those thoughts.[5] And the same is true for almost all difficult emotions. Naming them and talking about them openly helps; it doesn't hurt. After all, it's not like you can actually distract people from the biggest thing going on in their head at the moment.

That being said, if you are in a state of despair and people try to make you feel better by saying that they also feel gloomy from time to time, you have our permission to roll your eyes. In San Francisco, Mollie was not just "a little blue." She felt like she was drowning, with no hope of coming up for air.

Despair is often more than can be handled with just the support of friends and family, but it's exactly the kind of emotion that therapists, social workers, psychologists, and psychiatrists are trained to deal with. You might worry about sharing your despair with them, afraid that these emotions will be "too much." But that's what mental health professionals are there for.

Myth #2: Your life is too good for you to be feeling despair

Have you ever asked yourself, "Why do I feel so bad when other people objectively have it worse?" and then immediately felt ten times more awful? While writing this book, we often found ourselves starting sentences with "We know we're lucky to lead relatively great lives. . . ." But when we judge ourselves for feeling despair, we only sink deeper into the darkness.

Mollie often tried to remind herself that she was not getting tortured in prison or struggling with a drug addiction. But those thoughts did not make her feel better; they made her feel ungrateful and weak. When she finally gathered the courage to call her friend Julia, a licensed social worker, and confess through sobs how low, and yet guilty for feeling low, she felt, Julia interrupted her: "I don't believe in comparing levels of suffering. When you're in a low place, that's the place you're in."

Despair is absolute to the person who's in it. If you're struggling, you're struggling. There is no grand judge who gets to decide whether or not you "deserve" to feel despair. Yes, there are almost certainly other people in the world who objectively have it much, much worse than you do. You can still be suffering, and your feelings are still valid and important.

The following phrases are usually an indication that the person saying them is not equipped to support you. We know from experience that it's difficult to unhear these phrases and to stop them from making your stomach twist with guilt or anger (or both). Try not to take them to heart.

- "At least you don't . . ."
- "I know exactly how you feel, because I have dealt with [something not at all similar]."
- "I know someone who dealt with something similar, and I was amazed at how well she handled it."
- "I'm sure you'd feel better if you'd just . . ."
- "What if you just thought about it from a different perspective?"
- "Look on the bright side . . ."

If you have said any of these things to others, consider apologizing. Mollie had a friend in college who dealt with depression, and Mollie said something to her at the time along the lines of "What if you just stop fixating on everything that could go wrong?" In retrospect, this was not helpful. Mollie called her friend recently (fourteen years later) to say she was sorry, which her friend appreciated.

Myth #3: Despair is permanent, and it means your brain is broken

Y ou know, either everyone feels like this a little bit and they're just not talking about it, or I am completely fucking alone," Phoebe Waller-Bridge's
character sobs in the TV show *Fleabag*. "Which really isn't fucking funny."

When you're going through it, you may feel like you're the only one in the
world who isn't thriving. As we mentioned in chapter 2, we tend to compare our
behind-the-scenes footage with other people's highlight reels. If it seems (falsely)
that everyone else is thriving 24/7, it's easy to think that, because you're alone in
feeling so low, something must be deeply wrong with you and it will be wrong
with you forever.

But you're far from the only one grappling with despair. Mollie found it comforting when her therapist and her doctor both shared that suicidal feelings are
more common than society is willing to admit—and that many people do recover from these feelings. It's just that when we think having these thoughts
makes us so troubled that we will never be understood or accepted by others, we
refrain from sharing them with others. And when we don't share them with
others, we prevent ourselves from getting two things: one, the knowledge that
others have had these thoughts and that the thoughts have eventually passed,

and two, the help that we need to process our rumination so that it doesn't turn into action.

HOW IT FEELS   **WHAT'S POSSIBLE**

Whether your despair manifests as "I don't want to live" or "I can't imagine doing this job for another month, but I have no alternative" or "I don't have anyone in my life who loves me," those are the kinds of feelings that we're often not encouraged to talk about openly. So when we do experience them, we haven't had a chance to prepare or learn from others in our lives who may have gone through them in the past. As a result, we're often shocked at how horrific despair feels. How could there possibly be a purpose in feeling this bad? How could we possibly survive feeling this bad?

. . .

MOLLIE: *I struggled with suicidal thoughts for several months, although they were never as intense as they were that night in San Francisco. My thoughts from that night scared me enough to open up to my husband and therapist. I told them that I didn't want to take action to kill myself but that I also didn't want to be alive. My husband helped me by listening nonjudgmentally (while being firm that taking my life was not okay), even though I know I scared him, and my therapist helped me understand the desire behind my behavior. She described it as "looking over the edge and deciding whether I wanted to go there."*

Eventually, after I had looked over the edge long enough, I decided I didn't want to make that choice. The thought of throwing myself in front of a train still brought some relief, but I wasn't making active plans.

Sometimes all it takes is a single sentence to keep us alive. When I told my therapist I wanted to give up, she said, "That doesn't sound like you; that doesn't sound like the Mollie I know." I thought about that sentence a lot, and it helped keep me going. Someone I know who was struggling with suicidal thoughts was helped when his therapist simply said to him, "If you were gone, I'd miss you."

Medication helped. I went on the same antidepressant that a relative had used, which had helped them. It was also immensely helpful to hear from other people who had had these thoughts and had come out the other side. I listened to the author Parker Palmer talk on a podcast about how all he could do during his depression was go on walks in the middle of the night, when no one could see him. I listened to writer Andrew Solomon's experience of his suicidal thoughts: "One aspect of depression is a deep knowledge that the comforting doctors who assure you that your judgment is bad are wrong. You are in touch with the real terribleness of your life."⁶ I read Faith *by Sharon Salzberg and* When Things Fall Apart *by Pema Chödrön. And I spoke with three friends who had been through suicidal thoughts before. As I silently whimpered on the phone, unable to tell them in full sentences how bad it was, they said, "I know. I know. I'm here."*

For months, I wondered: Who are you when you no longer want to live? When the details of your life are too hard to bear? And what I can tell you about that horrific time was this: Some days it's enough to make it to bedtime—or even just after dinner—and to have pushed away the thoughts that have been nagging you all day, telling you it will never get better so what's the point. It's enough to be able to stop crying for a few minutes and splash water on your face as you notice that your eyelids have blistered from the tears that won't stop. It's enough to climb into bed and turn your electric heating pad on and close your eyes and hope that tomorrow might be a little bit better, and to be able to fall asleep only by imagining a thin web of humanity connecting you to everyone else who is currently suffering. Some days, that's all you can give, and I am here to say that that is enough. To you, in the middle of it, it may not feel like enough to stay alive, but I promise it is.

I kept hoping that a miracle would occur, that I would wake up and be out of pain, or I would find a doctor who would believe me or cure me. But of course none of these things happened, so I would lose hope. I finally let go of searching for hope, turned inward, and found faith within myself. Even if I didn't know what hope looked like yet, I clung to the belief that I would eventually find a way to move forward.

HOW TO WORK THROUGH IT

When it comes to despair, there are no shortcuts. Getting to a better place can be a painful process, and it may take months or years. But you *can* move through despair. You may even stumble upon moments of lightness while doing so. In this section, we'll first help you survive in the moment. We'll then offer guidance on how to rediscover hope, find emotional support, and slowly but steadily emerge from the darkness.

1. All you have to do is get through the now

Despair can make an evening feel endless. On the days when Mollie's chronic pain and depression were at their worst, she often found herself at 4 P.M. thinking, "I just have to be awake for five more hours. I think I can do that."

Focusing only on getting through what feels doable is called *chunking time*. The more you're suffering, the smaller the bits of time you need to chunk. "During a really difficult period, I scrapped the saying 'Take it day by day,'" reader Caroline told us. "Instead, I told myself to take it moment by moment."[7]

We also recommend indulging yourself, as long as what you choose to do isn't harmful. You'll often find that the part of you that experiences pleasure has not been completely extinguished. Pick a creature comfort and get lost in it: think ice cream sundaes, fluffy movies, or hot showers. It can also be helpful to find a long novel or, if you can't focus on reading (Mollie couldn't read a book for months), try a seven-season TV show to use as an extended escape. "Binging Netflix gives me breathing room from my own feelings when I need it," our friend Candice told us.

You may find that what you previously thought of as frivolous brings you peace. While she was struggling with despair, our friend Sophia, who never really liked animals, started to enjoy being around her neighbors' dogs. She also slept more, and spent hours in the evenings and mornings lying in bed and cocooning from the world. When reader Megan felt low for months, she bought herself a teddy bear to clutch while she marathoned the TV show *The Great British Bake Off*.

Finally, recognize that it's okay to have strong emotions or an extreme lack of emotions, and take note of how your moods ebb and flow. You may have a terrible morning but then have a better afternoon. "Feelings are actually more like weather systems—they blow in and they blow out," writes therapist Lori Gottlieb in her book *Maybe You Should Talk to Someone*.[8] Even if it feels like a lost cause, commit to chunking time and waiting it out to see if you feel a smidge better in ten minutes, or the next morning, or next week. One bad day, or even month, is not necessarily predictive of an eternal downward spiral.

Grief

Toward the end of his ten-year battle with cancer, Liz's father-in-law, Nikolai, suffered a stroke that left him unable to speak or move.

Nikolai, a Russian folksinger, had always been the life of the party. When he was checked into the hospital over the holidays, he had his room decorated with twinkling lights and had holiday tunes played on the accordion. The nurses regularly stopped by to join him in singing "We Wish You a Merry Christmas" and "Dreidel, Dreidel, Dreidel."

After Liz's last words to him, with great effort, he managed to raise his hands in the air and give one small, final wave. The next day at 3 A.M., he passed away.

In the wake of a loss, the world stops. There is no escaping the emptiness and the agony. In this way, grief is similar to despair: you simply come undone. Life is drained of color, and you have to force yourself through the day.

Fully delving into grief requires much more than a sidebar (see "Resources on grief" on pages 236–37), but we do want to call out a few things:

- Remember that feeling shattered is normal. The pain won't go away, but it will lessen over the years.
- Grief can crystallize what matters most. Write it down so that when you return to your day-to-day, you don't forget. After Nikolai's death, Liz sent herself an email in which she wrote, "Live a big, ridiculous life. If you can make an ordinary moment magical or cinematic, do it. Have a family. Learn to play the accordion, and bust it out at every holiday."
- Sharing stories with others can help, especially stories of the good times.
- You can experience joy and grief at the same time. You may find yourself bent over with laughter as you recount a memory, and then unable to stop yourself from breaking down.
- The five stages of grief (denial, anger, bargaining, depression, acceptance) are more of a messy cycle than a sequential progression (and some even consider them up for debate).
- Researchers have now added a sixth stage to grief: meaning. Remember that meaning is personal and can take time. "Even though you find meaning, it is not worth the cost of losing someone," says grief and loss expert David Kessler. "But in time, meaningful connections may replace painful memories. You will be able to focus on the meaning rather than the horrible aspects of a loved one dying."[9]

- You may feel a newfound sense of spirituality. Embrace it. Liz, who has never been religious, found it impossible that a personality as large as Nikolai's would just suddenly be nowhere. She doesn't know exactly what she believes, but she does think he lives on in some way.
- You might experience moments when you feel like you're bursting with a renewed appreciation of life. Lean into those feelings. Life is short. Have some fun with it.

THE PROGRESSION OF GRIEF

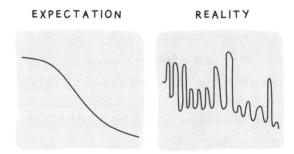

EXPECTATION   REALITY

We'll leave you with a description of grief by a Reddit user in 2011 that brought Liz a lot of comfort:

> You'll find it comes in waves. When the ship is first wrecked, you're drowning, with wreckage all around you. . . . For a while, all you can do is float. Stay alive. In the beginning, the waves are 100 feet tall and crash over you without mercy. They come 10 seconds apart and don't even give you time to catch your breath. After a while, maybe weeks, maybe months,

you'll find the waves are still 100 feet tall, but they come further apart. When they come, they still crash all over you and wipe you out. But in between, you can breathe, you can function. . . . The waves never stop coming, and somehow you don't really want them to. But you learn that you'll survive them. And other waves will come. And you'll survive them too.[10]

2. Set yourself small daily intentions

When you're in despair, there's so much that you wish were going better. For months before the night in San Francisco, Mollie felt like she was in free fall: every day was worse than the last, and her suicidal thoughts were getting more intense. It was as if she had descended into a canyon and didn't know when she would hit the bottom, or what her personal version of bottoming out would look like. That's the scary part: on the plummet into despair, it feels like you are losing all control. Your mental state has collapsed, and so it can be overwhelming to try to take on everything (or even anything).

Here's the first thing that helped: when you are in free fall, all you have to do is throw a single climbing pick into the wall every day. This will not stop the fall, but it will slow it. Each morning, choose one thing you'll accomplish that day. Your goal can be as simple as sending a single text, taking out the trash, or putting on deodorant.

These small acts serve an important function: they put you back in the driver's seat of your life, even if it's just for a few minutes. Setting yourself even the smallest goal and achieving it can help you start to move toward a more hopeful future. Mollie had a tendency to brush mini-milestones aside—*Okay, so I went to the drugstore today. That's my accomplishment? In comparison with what I used to be able to do in a day, that's nothing. Who am I kidding?* But over the course of weeks and months, her small actions added up. Slowly, she felt her

BIG STEPS WHEN YOU FEEL DESPAIR

DOING THE LAUNDRY

TAKING A BATH

SOME FORM OF EXERCISE

EATING A HEALTHY MEAL

REPLYING TO A TEXT

HAVING THE COURAGE TO ASK FOR HELP

independence, courage, and hope start to return. At first it felt like ten steps backward, one step forward. And then two steps back, one forward. And then, after a few months, she started inching upward from the abyss.

If you're having trouble getting started, it might help to put yourself on autopilot. "When I had no energy to do anything, I pretended I was a character in a video game," reader Sam told us. This type of distancing technique can reduce the intensity of your emotions and make it easier to take action. "Video-game me had to take a shower," Sam recalled, "so I just sort of watched my body turn the nozzle and stand there. And then eventually my mind caught up and realized that the hot water felt good."[11]

You can also leave yourself reminders. A few months after the night in San Francisco, Mollie joined a group of women in her temple who met monthly to work together to cultivate personal traits in a practice called Mussar. They studied the traits and supported one another to take small steps toward bringing them into their daily and weekly routines. Mollie chose *savlanut* (Hebrew for "patience"), which is defined as "opening the space between the match and the fuse," and bearing without suffering.[12] She taped a notecard with these words onto her computer and found comfort in viewing this as a trait that could be practiced.

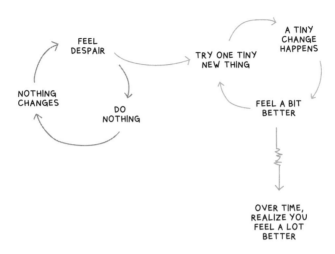

3. Reach out to people who get it

In the summer of 2020, our friends Kate and Hunter learned that their unborn baby had a rare syndrome that involved heart and brain malformations. After consulting with their doctors, family, and friends, they made the agonizing decision to terminate the pregnancy.[13]

In the wake of their loss, Kate and Hunter were devastated. To help them process their despair, Kate's family gifted them a weekend away at a seaside cottage. "We walked to a nearby lighthouse in the middle of the night," Kate recalled. "We found a bench, and in the darkness, we grieved and asked our baby for forgiveness."

In the following months, Kate started to talk every day with a friend who had also terminated a pregnancy for medical reasons. "Because she had gone through the same thing," Kate told us, "we were able to offer each other judgment-free support. Abortion is such a hot-button issue, and I was sometimes afraid of how people might react. But with her, I didn't have to worry that I was going to say the wrong thing. Our shared experience gave me the courage to reach out whenever I wanted, and to be completely open about how I was feeling."

Kate and Hunter also joined a support group for people who had gone through similar situations. "It was so nice to have a block of time to talk about what we had gone through and to know we would be heard and understood. Even if they hadn't been through the exact same thing, people just got it. We didn't have to defend or explain our decision; there was just this immediate sense of compassion."

From time to time, Kate will still read posts on a related Facebook group to feel less alone. "I'm realizing I will never get over this," she admitted to us. "But reaching out to people who have been through the same thing has helped me realize that the despair will persist but evolve. The connections and support have been an opportunity to hold grief and joy at once."

One of Liz's favorite sayings is "A problem shared is a problem halved." In the midst of despair, we often feel an urge to isolate ourselves. But while retreating from the world may feel protective in the moment, talking to people who have gone through something similar can be a powerful step toward recovery (Caveat: You are the one who decides whether or not another person gets it. You may have friends or family who are well-meaning but unable to fully understand or support you.)

And remember: when you share a tough emotion, you don't have to present it in a perfectly edited form or add any caveats. As blogger Molly Flinkman writes, we often say something like "Oh, I'm pretty tired. Still adjusting to the newborn schedule," when we mean "I cry constantly all day and all night—it's a miracle I'm not crying right now—because this child won't sleep unless she's being held. Also breastfeeding is so painful that I have taken up middle-of-the-night cursing to cope."[14] She calls this "polished pain," and it doesn't serve us well. The people who care about you will welcome the truth—and greet you with the same honesty and vulnerability.

In some cases, our isolation isn't self-imposed: we feel despair because isolation is being forced on us by others. While working at a nonprofit, reader Gina was harassed and ostracized by her coworkers. Her self-confidence took such a

hit that when her bosses told her that no one else would ever want to hire her, she believed them and plunged into despair. She felt stuck in a job that was wreaking havoc on her mental health, and powerless to improve her situation.

In desperation, Gina joined a social club for women. Attending events helped her start to form connections outside the nonprofit sector. And as she spoke to other members about her current work and her professional aspirations, she was greeted not only with emotional support but also with new job opportunities. Eventually, Gina was able to transition to a new role and company where she is much happier. Something similar happened to Mollie. When she finally opened up about her chronic pain after a year and a half of hiding it, a friend connected her with a former classmate who had gone through something similar. Mollie emailed her, and she sent back an enlightening article from *The New Yorker* about chronic pain.

The someone who gets it might even be a some*thing*. While on vacation, Mollie limped a short distance in the Olympic National Forest to see the oldest Sitka spruce in the world. As she gazed up at the thousand-year-old tree, she felt a sense of peace. "It has lived to see ten of our lives," she thought. Whatever troubles Mollie was having seemed less overpowering in the context of the vast history of life on earth.

What to do if someone experiencing despair reaches out to you

If someone opens up to you, they've likely been struggling with whether or not they should say something for a while. First and foremost, make them feel safe. Listen without judgment and avoid jumping into "fix it" mode. It's not that making suggestions is inherently bad, but using phrases like "If you'd just" or "Have you tried" implies that if only the person tried a little harder, did a little more research, or were a little more capable, the problem could be easily fixed.

Instead, reassure them and provide comfort. Here are some phrases to try:

- "Even though I don't know firsthand what you're going through, I want you to know that I care about you."
- "Is there something I can do to help, or would you like me to just listen?"
- "I really want to know what's going on, even if it's hard."

Many people in states of despair would like to shift their perspective, but they can't, hence the despair. Sometimes these shifts can take years, even with the help of a good therapist, so be prepared and be open to listen to someone struggling with despair more than once.

You can go even further by offering specific, small ways that you might be able to support them. When Liz's father-in-law died, her friend Logan texted her: "Here are four things I'd love to do for you. Let me know which one(s) might feel good, and when you'd like to do it. 1) I can call you and just listen, 2) I can bake and bring your favorite dessert, 3) I can be here on text whenever you need to vent but don't have the energy for a phone call, 4) I can come over and walk around the block with you." The text made Liz feel supported and also affirmed that she could reach out to Logan without worrying that she'd be a burden.

And finally, show that you value their existence by continuing to check in on them. They might not have the energy to reach out to you, but we've heard many stories about how a text as simple as "No need to reply, just wanted to let you know I'm thinking of you" meant the world to someone.

4. Distance yourself from people who don't get it

"There are so many people who are afraid to voice that they need help," Meghan Markle told Oprah during an interview in March 2021, "and I know how hard it is to not just voice it but to be told no." After marrying Prince Harry and joining the British royal family, Meghan became the target of racist bullying online and from the press. She told Oprah she wasn't allowed to leave her home and began to have "real and frightening" thoughts. At one point, Meghan "just didn't want to be alive anymore."

When she finally gathered the courage to ask for help, the British royal family refused to do anything—or even to let Meghan go elsewhere for support. It would be unacceptable, they told her. "It was very scary, and I didn't know who to turn to," Meghan admitted, adding that she confided in Harry and eventually turned to Princess Diana's best friends, "because who else could understand what it's actually like on the inside?" Eventually, she and Harry decided to step back from their senior royal positions and move to the United States.

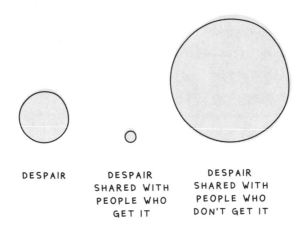

DESPAIR

DESPAIR
SHARED WITH
PEOPLE WHO
GET IT

DESPAIR
SHARED WITH
PEOPLE WHO
DON'T GET IT

While we recommend reaching out for social and emotional support, be careful to reach out to the right people, especially when it comes to issues of identity. For some trans and nonbinary people, long periods of their lives are marked by severe despair. And this cloud of despair may only begin to lift when they either meet another trans person or even just begin researching gender on the internet. Those tiny moments of connection and understanding can be a lifeline; however, first telling someone who is not accepting can be difficult. When musical artist Summer Luk came out as transgender to her parents at age twenty-one, they rejected her. On the phone, they told Summer that she wasn't their daughter and would always be their son, and then hung up on her. Summer felt deep anger toward her family (though she is now working on her relationship with them) and so tried to build and find community elsewhere, first by writing and performing music in New York City. "As I tell my story through music, it somehow becomes a bridge for the audience to relate to me," she wrote in *Teen Vogue*. "People would come up to tell me that my story humanized an experience that they thought was outside them."[15] She also found strength online in places like TikTok, where she posts content about being a trans woman. "It's always scary to share your story as someone who belongs to a marginalized community and it's great to see so many people relating, supporting and sharing my content!"[16] If you're struggling with despair related to a facet of your identity, it can be helpful to first find support from a community of people who get it (whether in person or online).

Look for people who can offer you *empathy* instead of sympathy. As Brené Brown explains, empathy is when someone tries to understand you so they can figure out how to be helpful. For example, when Liz learned about Mollie's severe foot pain, she sent her a bag of activities to do inside that did not involve using her feet. Sympathy, on the other hand, is looking down at someone from a better place. Another way to think of it is that empathy is saying, "Yes, I know how hard that is," while sympathy is "You poor thing, I wish there was something I could do." If you find that friends are being sympathetic and not empathetic, it's okay to take a break from those friendships for a while.

If you need to maintain distance from someone, try naming your emotions and then setting a kind but firm boundary. "I'm going through a really hard time, and I love you," Mollie told a friend, "but I don't have the capacity to talk to you as frequently as we used to. I hope you can understand." Her friend appreciated the honesty and that Mollie didn't disappear without an explanation.

While we wish all our friends could be empathetic, the truth is, some of them haven't gone through anything hard yet, and some of them are better suited for times in our lives when things are going well. Friendships can wax and wane if we give them the space to do so, and just because you experience distance at some point doesn't mean you'll never be close again.

Understanding chronic health issues and invisible conditions

When Mollie was going through the worst of her pain, she reached out to her husband's aunt, Judy Cohen. Judy is a transformation coach who is a cancer survivor and a late-deafened adult and who also lives with a difficult chronic health condition. Judy told Mollie about the Spoon Theory, created by Christine Miserandino, who has lupus.[17]

The story goes like this: Miserandino was eating at a diner with a friend and went to take her lupus medicine. Her friend asked what it felt like to live with a chronic illness. Miserandino picked up the spoons from their own table and others and asked her friend to imagine that the spoons represent the amount of physical and mental energy a person has on any given day. If you're healthy, you have an unlimited number of spoons. "Most people start the day with an unlimited [number] of possibilities," Miserandino writes, "and energy to do whatever they desire, especially young people. For the most part, they do not need to worry about the effects of their actions."

People who are dealing with a chronic health condition only have a limited number of spoons, and throughout their day, every action takes away spoons until there are no more spoons. When they plan their day, they need to know exactly how many "spoons" they're starting with and then keep track throughout the day. They can never not think about their spoons. Not sleeping well takes away a spoon, getting ready for work takes away a spoon, commuting takes away a spoon. If you want more spoons, you can't get them. If you run out, you are done for the day and need to rest.

"Sometimes you can borrow against tomorrow's 'spoons,' but just think how hard tomorrow will be with [fewer] 'spoons,'" she writes. "A person who is sick always lives with the looming thought that tomorrow may be the day that a cold comes, or an infection, or any number of things that could be very dangerous. So you do not want to run low on 'spoons,' because you never know when you truly will need them."

This is difficult for people with unlimited spoons to understand, especially in relation to people who "look okay." People who don't have invisible conditions, whether mental or physical, often struggle to understand people who do. Author Meghan O'Rourke, who suffers from an autoimmune disorder, writes, "One of the hardest things about being chronically ill is that most people find what you're going through incomprehensible—if they [even] believe you are going through it. In your loneliness, your preoccupation with an enduring new reality, you want to be understood in a way that you can't be."[18]

If you are friends with someone who has limited spoons, ask them if they feel comfortable sharing with you what their days are like, so you can better understand. See "Resources on chronic pain" on page 237. Also check out the #spoonie hashtag on social media.

5. Let go of "being on track"

Most of us have a mental checklist for how we expect our lives to progress. Even if no specifics come to mind, you probably still have a vague notion that you'll move through different stages as you get older.

But our plans can evaporate overnight. Events that we tend to associate with old age, like death or illness, can happen at any time. And when they do hit us earlier in life, we're often left feeling isolated, because so few of our peers can relate. Our friend Andrew underwent a year of chemotherapy at age thirty-six and moved to be closer to the treatment center. "I'm shuttling between the hospital and a barren apartment while everyone I know is getting promoted and going to house parties," he once told Liz. "No one really gets it. Sometimes I even think people have forgotten about what's happening to me." Several readers we spoke with went through an early divorce or stayed single until later in life and felt out of step. When we miss out on going through major life milestones with our peers, it can feel like we are no longer "on track."

But when you endure despair at a younger age, you may acquire tools that will serve you for the rest of your life. Glynnis MacNicol, who documented her experience of accepting that she was choosing to be permanently single and childless in her book *No One Tells You This*, wrote about how alone she felt in her thirties when her friends were all getting married and having children. But in her forties, some of her friends got divorced or had other major life issues, and she was the first person they came to. MacNicol was good at helping others move through difficult times. "Life comes back around, and back around again if you let it," she writes. "People leave, but they also come back."[19]

Author Sarah Manguso dealt with chronic inflammatory demyelinating polyneuropathy (CIPD), a neurological disease, for years in her twenties, which forced her to "yield control to a force greater than my will." In *Ongoingness*, she wrote that her experiences—"diagnoses, deaths, unbreakable vows—weren't the beginnings or the ends of anything." Instead, Manguso focused on an unending life force that she was simply a part of. "I could imagine my will as a force that would not disappear but redistribute when I died, and that all life contained the same force, and that I needn't worry about my impending death because the great responsibility of my life was to contain the force for a while and then relinquish it."[20] Zooming out from your life to the cosmic forces can let you unclench your control, even just for a moment.

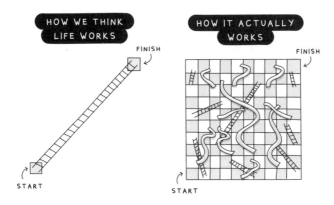

6. **Make meaning out of it**

"I'm tired. . . . I'm frustrated. I'm sick," wrote Joy Ekuta in a *Medium* post on June 2, 2020. "I'm exhausted."[21] COVID had all but shut down the events company she had founded the previous year. Quarantine had left her feeling isolated in her West Oakland, California, apartment. And the week before, George Floyd's cruel murder at the hands of a white police officer in Minneapolis had sparked global demonstrations.

Joy, a Black woman, was part of a Slack group with many of her Black friends. "We were all talking about how tired we were," she told us. "Tired of watching the news, tired of feeling desensitized, tired of hearing from people. And we all just thought maybe we should do something for us."[22] When a few people suggested hosting a Juneteenth celebration, the group realized many of them didn't really know many details about what it stood for—that it was first celebrated by formerly enslaved Black Texans on June 19, 1866, on the first anniversary of their finding out, two and a half years late, that slavery had been abolished.[23] Joy and her friends decided to put together hellajuneteenth.com, a website that would help people learn about the holiday and encourage them to celebrate it.

"Then we thought: We're going to take the day off. Could we encourage others to do the same? Wouldn't it be cool if we could get a bunch of companies involved?" The group started to circulate the website more widely.

When Twitter CEO Jack Dorsey tweeted a link to the site, "things just kind of snowballed from there," Joy told us. Over the next two weeks, more than 650 companies (including TikTok, McKinsey, Netflix, and Mastercard) publicly committed, on hellajuneteenth.com, to observing Juneteenth. Offers to help grow the movement poured in. A PR company took them on as a pro bono client, and the website-hosting service for hellajuneteenth waived its fees. On June 16, 2021, US President Joe Biden signed a bill into law making Juneteenth a national holiday.

As the movement grew, Joy and her friends were clear about setting boundaries. "We made the explicit choice to use whatever language we wanted and be clear about what our goal was. We all set out-of-office messages on June 19. A few companies wanted us to do live events with them on Juneteenth, but we said no. We really focused on our joy and just turned everything else off."

She added, "The fact that Juneteenth became a holiday, that will go on for years. That goes beyond our group of friends. We were able to create institutional change. It was really empowering."

When you're in the midst of despair, it's frustrating to hear that your experience may be helpful to others in the future. You'd rather not be helpful if it means you have to go through it. We find it insulting when people like self-help guru Tony Robbins suggest that we ask ourselves, "What's great about this?" Our situation is not always great. The point isn't to make it great. But it is happening, and so if it has to happen, it can be helpful to think about how to make meaning of your experience, either for yourself or for others.

Psychologists have determined that making meaning is a key stage in recovery. It helps us transition from isolation to finding a purpose—even if it's a seemingly small purpose, like showing up to a job or taking care of an animal—that can pull us through. Making meaning doesn't have to involve changing your career or starting a nonprofit. It can simply be a shift in how you relate to others. A large percentage of the population will feel despair at some point in their lives.

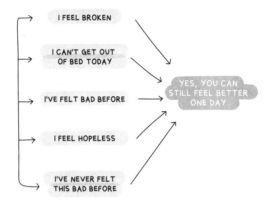

When you have been through it, you are better able to notice when others are not coping and to offer them comfort. "To go on going on . . . ," writes author Joan Chittister, "despite being clearly damaged, in full view of a world that sees us to have been wounded, is to discover what it really means to be human. It is also the moment in which we are given the opportunity to reinvent ourselves, to become the rest of what we are able to be."[24]

. . .

MOLLIE: *It's been more than two years since that night in San Francisco. As I look back at what helped me move out of the abyss, it wasn't one thing, and there wasn't a demarcation line after which everything was better. I let time pass. For a few months, I continued in a middle ground, teetering back and forth between despair and faith. Each new injury and source of physical pain was frustrating and did bring more despair, but also surprisingly brought hope, because I saw how healing was possible. Seeing one part of my body slowly heal convinced me that my feet could recover as well, given enough time and physical therapy.*

In finding a new job that I really liked, I was able to add more meaning to my day-to-day life, which helped give me a reason to get up in the morning. I didn't want to let my new team down, and I knew I could make a difference through my work. I started going to Shabbat services regularly and found meaning in faith. I started a book club of women whose connection provided comfort.

Things are still difficult today. I still have pain in multiple body parts. And I feel further away from having children than I ever have before, since I want to let my body heal first and then also have some time to live my life without pain before adding pregnancy and childbirth into the mix. I accept this, even though it is not what I wanted.

My husband, Chris, has had to play the role of caretaker for me and, at times, has had to let his career take a backseat. I am so thankful for his love as he has cooked, cleaned, and cared for me. None of this has been easy for him, either.

Now I look back at that dark time period with amazement. I realize that even though it felt endlessly monstrous, it was also a time of healing. I didn't know then how I'd find the strength to go on, but I did. I do want to live. As they say, I want to stay for the miracle.

Despair is hard. Life is hard. The daily nature of living can feel so interminable. There are days when I think about how much of life I still have to get through. But I promise you that you DO have the capacity to handle it, even if, at the moment, you don't know it yet.

TAKEAWAYS

- Working with a mental health professional can make a world of difference

- Don't judge yourself: if you're suffering, you're suffering
- To get through the day, chunk time and notice that your feelings can ebb and flow
- Set a (very) small goal for yourself each day
- Reach out to those who get it, and create distance from those who don't
- Let go of the idea that your life needs to follow a specific track
- Find meaning in your experience; what that looks like will vary from person to person

CHAPTER 7

Regret

Nothing can ever happen twice.
In consequence, the sorry fact is
that we arrive here improvised
and leave without the chance to practice.

Wisława Szymborska

LIZ: *I was formatting a spreadsheet at work when my mom called.*
"Oma passed away last night."

My grandmother lived to be a hundred, so her death was far from unexpected. But we were close, and I stayed with her almost every summer until I was a teenager.

My fondest childhood memories are set in my grandmother's house, which she designed and built for herself in a small village in Germany. I can still vividly picture the floral wallpaper in her bedroom, the worn knobs of her kitchen cabinets, and the geometric pattern of the rug I played on while my mom and grandmother sat behind me in big armchairs, sharing a bottle of wine and laughing. My grandmother's house was our connection to my mom's past and to my extended family. A place to call home in a country that otherwise felt foreign.

A few days later, my mom called again. She was going to Germany for two weeks to clean out the house and decide whether we should sell it or try to keep it. She hesitated for a moment. "Would you come with me?" It was a rare request.

I said I'd think about it and hung up. The timing seemed too stressful. I had just been staffed on a new project at work, and I was hoping to get promoted soon. Could I really afford to take two weeks off? Wouldn't I be seen as unreliable and lazy?

The next morning, I told her I couldn't go.

Writing this story makes my stomach lurch with guilt. I wish I had been there for my mom. I could have helped her pack everything up and slipped a trinket into my pocket as a souvenir. Maybe together, we could have figured out a way to keep the house. But none of that happened. The house is gone.

. . .

We feel regret when we think about how our lives could have been better had we only done something differently. It can overwhelm us, or seem like a burden we'll have to carry forever. Several readers we spoke with said they often felt mired in the past, stuck mentally replaying moments when they felt they had made the wrong decision.

But while regret can ache, it can also be a powerful internal compass for how to live an engaged, meaningful life. Learning from your past is one of the most effective ways to set yourself up for a better, less regret-filled future.

Before we get to all that, let's start with a few basics. Psychologists describe regret as a *counterfactual emotion*, a feeling that happens when we dream of what might have been had we chosen something else (the counterfactual). The amount of regret we feel depends on how close we came to realizing one of those alternate possibilities. If you're running to catch a train, and you miss it by a few seconds, you'll feel a lot more regret watching it pull out of the station than if you had arrived an hour late. Cornell psychologists found that bronze Olympic medalists were much happier than silver medalists, because the bronze medalists were thrilled to have gotten anything at all. The silver medalists just obsessed over how they could have gotten gold.[1]

Science also shows that no matter what we choose, we'll feel regret from time to time. Does that doom us to spend eternity slogging through endless what-might-have-beens? Not necessarily. And we have more good news (so please don't regret the fact that you started reading this chapter): you shouldn't *want* to completely stop pining over your past. Without feeling heartbroken over a lost opportunity or mistake, you wouldn't learn anything. "It's much better to wake up now in deep regret, desperate not to waste more of your life obsessing and striving for meaningless crap," writes author Anne Lamott in her book *Stitches*.[2]

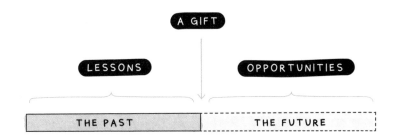

In this chapter, we'll walk you through common mistakes we tend to make about regret, outline six types of regret and how to handle and learn from each one, and then offer a few mind-set shifts and tactical tips for those inevitable moments of obsessing over what might have been.

MYTHS ABOUT REGRET

Myth #1: You can live a life of #NoRegrets

If you marry, you will regret it; if you do not marry, you will also regret it," wrote the Danish philosopher Søren Kierkegaard.[3]

We'd love to spill the secrets to living a #NoRegrets life, but we have bad news: it doesn't exist.

Obsessing over the past transcends age, race, culture, gender, and social status. Studies of day-to-day conversations show that people talk about regret more than any other emotion except love, and that regret is the uncomfortable emotion we feel most often.[4]

We're hardwired to feel regret. If your ancestor ate a bright red poisonous berry and spent the next twenty-four hours in gut-wrenching agony, it would be important for him to realize that he made the wrong decision. And it would be useful for him to vividly imagine how much better his life would have been if he had not eaten that red berry.

We can even feel regret when things work out for us. A few years ago, Liz's friend Erik placed a bet that, against all odds, won him a lot of money. He was overjoyed—and then lamented the fact that he hadn't bet even *more* money.

In fact, the cinematic moments we associate with a #NoRegrets life tend to be those in which we're most likely to ache for what might have been. Big life transitions, like moving, getting married, or switching jobs, involve committing to something, whether that's a city, a partner, or a company. They also mean *not* committing to a million other things. And so, at those pivotal moments, it's natural to fantasize about the million potential lives we're cutting off.

Myth #2: If you follow your passion, you'll never feel regret

I look at two of my closest friends, who are doctors," reader Nina, a teacher, told us. "I love my career, but I sometimes think, 'I could do what they do had I gone to med school.' But I didn't. And now I can't afford to buy a house in the same city as they did."

What you regret depends on which part of yourself you're tapping into. Some psychologists believe that we have three selves:

- The *actual self*—who you are right now
- The *ideal self*—the truest, most fulfilled version of you
- The *ought self*—the you that would check off all of society's boxes[5]

These selves will each feel different regrets. If you accept a prestigious but soul-sucking job, your ideal self might be miserable, but your ought self will be on top of the world; and if you decide to turn it down, the reverse will be true. That's because, deep down, you might want two different things.

So where does that leave you?

In general, studies show that we are much happier when we pick what we're passionate about over what we think we *should* do. But even if you craft a life that you love, you'll likely still have moments when your ought self hijacks your brain and makes you feel bad. Just knowing what's happening can help you accept and normalize those inevitable moments—and make it easier to bounce back. "I'm the only one of my siblings who chose not to have kids," reader Jack shared with us. "And sometimes when I play with my two-year-old niece, I find myself wondering, 'What if?' But I feel confident in my decision, so I don't put much weight on those thoughts when they pop up."

Myth #3: Always pick the option you'll regret least

When it comes to decision making, a reasonable strategy is to imagine which option will make us feel the least regret and to then pick that option.

But exactly *when* you imagine you'll feel that regret matters a lot. Too often, we focus on the short term. Looking for a different job will be time-consuming and stressful. Breaking up with our live-in partner will involve complicated logistics. Taking two weeks off of work when you've just been put on a new project and feel the need to prove yourself will be too stressful.

But avoiding regret in the next hour, day, or month tends to lead us down a path we regret more in the long run. We stay in a job we hate for years. We shy away from uncertainty to such an extent that we settle for a relationship that isn't fulfilling. We don't go on that once-in-a-lifetime trip with our mom.

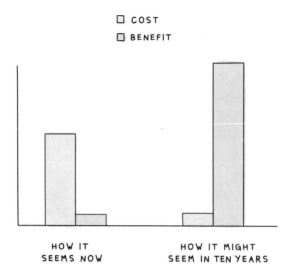

☐ COST
☐ BENEFIT

HOW IT
SEEMS NOW

HOW IT MIGHT
SEEM IN TEN YEARS

Our tendency to avoid immediate discomfort is called the *status quo bias*. Making a change involves risk and uncertainty, so we often do nothing when we'd be better off trying something new. Researchers have found that *feeling regret* and *being afraid* of feeling regret activate the same parts of the brain.[6] In other words, your fear of making the wrong decision can be as painful as actually dealing with the consequences of your actions (more on what to do with all this in the next section).

• • •

LIZ: *My father-in-law died when I was thirty-two, and it made me see my grandmother's death completely differently. I hadn't understood how destabilizing it feels to lose a parent, no matter how old they are or how old you are, until he passed. In the days following his death, I thought often of my mom, surrounded by strangers on an eight-hour flight, counting down the hours until she would have to neatly pack away her own mother's life.*

I would give up a lot to go back, make a different decision, and be with her at that moment. The only thing I can do now is be better at putting the people I love first. When my father-in-law died, I didn't think twice about taking bereavement leave. For a week, I ignored my email. Instead, I coordinated with the funeral director, filled our fridge with food, and drafted an obituary. I tried to take as many logistics off of my husband's plate as possible.

When my own dad was rushed to the hospital with heart issues, my mom tried to reassure me. They were in the suburbs of Chicago, and I was living two thousand miles away, in San Francisco. "You don't have to come home. I know how busy you are. We'll be fine."

I didn't listen to her. I immediately got on a plane and went home. A week later, as I flopped down next to my mom on her bed, she took my hand. "I'm so glad you're here," she told me. I was glad, too. I squeezed her hand.

HOW TO WORK THROUGH IT

Fully experienced, [regret] turns our eyes, attentive and alert, to a future possibly lived better than our past," writes the poet David Whyte.[7]

When you look back, what do you regret most?

Answering this question can teach you about yourself and what you care about—even more than examining your past achievements. Neuroimaging shows that when we feel regret, the parts of our brain associated with reasoning light up.[8] Examining our regrets helps us make sense of our lives and gives us an opportunity to pinpoint what we'd like to change. Researchers find that people tend to value regret partly because it helps them remedy what went wrong.[9]

In this section, we'll walk you through six types of regret, help you identify and explore each one, and then leave you with broader advice on making peace with your if-onlys.

WHEN YOU DIVE INTO
YOUR REGRETS...

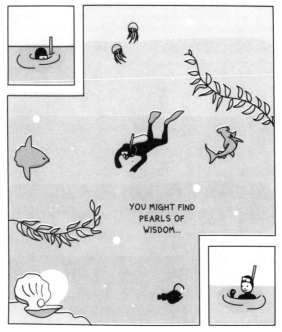

YOU MIGHT FIND
PEARLS OF
WISDOM...

...JUST MAKE
SURE TO COME
BACK UP AGAIN

1. Allow yourself to grieve what wasn't

But first: While regret is often the doorway to a better way of being, it can also be gut-wrenching. Even if you're able to learn from your past or make amends for mistakes, you may still have moments when you feel bowled over by sorrow.

It's okay to grieve.

As with all big feelings, the best way to handle regret is to sit with the heartache. That means allowing yourself to cry or curl up in bed for a while if you feel like it.

When we spoke with readers about regret, many mentioned losing something that they could never recover: time, their youth, the chance to say "I love you" or "I'm sorry" to someone before they passed away. There is no way to feel "good" about these missed opportunities. Many also told us about making decisions to do things they shouldn't have. But whatever the specific regret, all of them told us that the depth of their pain gave them the motivation to do better next time. Everyone pointed to the moment of acceptance, of letting themselves finally face their anguish, as a turning point for positive change.

The rest of this chapter will focus on how to move on. But know that it's normal to find the path forward bumpy. In one of her most popular "Dear Sugar" columns, author Cheryl Strayed writes that each of us must contend with "the ghost ship that didn't carry us."[10] You stand on the ship that is your life and watch the ghost ship—all the choices you didn't make—sail away. That ship is "important and beautiful," but it's not yours. All you can do is learn to gracefully "salute it from the shore." In order to accept the choices we *did* make, Strayed also suggests that we ask ourselves, "What if all those things I shouldn't have done were what got me here? What if I was never redeemed? What if I already was?"[11]

2. Understand what type of regret you are experiencing

Start by categorizing your regrets into one (or more) of these six buckets:

- **Hindsight regrets:** you made the best decision that you could then, but you know more now
- **Alternate-self regrets:** you have a vague sense of regret that comes from wanting to live different lives
- **Rushing-in regrets:** you made a decision that you weren't sure about or weren't ready to make at the time
- **Dragging-out regrets:** you waffled about a decision for a long time, even though you sort of knew what you needed to do

- **Ignoring-your-instincts regrets:** you had a gut feeling that you weren't making the right decision but acquiesced to others' needs or opinions
- **Self-sabotage regrets:** you made a decision that you knew wasn't good for you, but you did it to protect yourself from feeling another emotion (rejection, loneliness, vulnerability)

For the **first two types of regret**, your best bet is to distract yourself and remove your rose-colored glasses about what could have been. For the **last four types of regret**, you'll want to spend a bit more time analyzing the regret so it can help you change your future behavior.

Hindsight regrets revolve around a choice that led to a situation you couldn't have predicted. When you find yourself saying, "If I had known then what I know now . . . ," you're experiencing a hindsight regret.

In his memoir, *Saturday Night Live* (*SNL*) head writer Colin Jost recalls a time when his father left a job that he loved for another that seemed promising but ended up being awful. The depth of his father's depression after the job switch made Jost wary of moving on from *SNL* whenever he thought about trying something new, yet he understands why his father went for what, at the time, seemed like "a huge opportunity."[12]

If you thought carefully before making a decision but things didn't go as well as you'd hoped, that doesn't reveal a personal failing or much information about what to do differently in the future. Jost's father had no way of knowing exactly what his day-to-day at the new workplace would be like or how things would evolve over time. While it's easy to look back and think that the "right" decision was obvious, remind yourself that you did the best you could given what you knew.

What to do about it: For hindsight regrets, ask yourself:

- Was there any way I could have foreseen these conditions?
- Was my decision justifiable, because I was making it based on incomplete information I was given or during uncertain conditions?

- Can I acknowledge that sometimes good decisions have bad outcomes for which I am not to blame?

Remind yourself that your coulda-woulda-shoulda thoughts exist only because you can look back and see what happened *after* the fact. Maybe you were young. Or you had no way of knowing what the next day would bring. The point is, if you were plopped back into the same situation with the same information, chances are you would do the same thing.

Alternate-self regrets are the vague pangs we feel when we think about all the lives we will never lead. Picking one option inevitably moves us away from a different option.

CAUTION:
THINGS WERE NOT AS OBVIOUS
AS THEY APPEAR IN HINDSIGHT

It's useful to keep in mind that we tend to romanticize our could-have-been lives. A few years ago, Liz found a comfy-looking mint-green armchair on Craigslist. She returned to the listing a couple times every day for a week and emailed the seller, but she couldn't commit. She decided not to buy it, and a week later, the listing was gone.

For over a year, Liz fantasized about how nice her apartment would have looked with the mint-green chair.

And then the chair reappeared on Craigslist. But instead of jumping on it, as she had imagined she would, Liz realized she had been right not to buy it the first time. She wasn't really that jazzed about it. And poof: her fantasies evaporated.

What to do about it: When you're deep in the throes of imagining an alternate life, chances are you're romanticizing it. In Liz's mind, the mint-green chair grew to become a magical, constant source of happiness that had slipped through her fingers. In reality, Liz didn't actually like the chair that much. She also reminded herself of other purchases that had given her blips of joy but never any long-lasting sense of fulfillment. Thinking more specifically through your imagined alternate realities can help snap you out of your fantasy.

You can live only one life. There's no Undo or Restart button. You can let that reality tear you up, or you can look at it as Liz does. She and her husband have talked about the infinite lives they each might have lived—and 99 percent don't have the other person in them. Liz and her husband could still, at any moment, choose a life without the other person. But they don't. And that makes the choice all the more special.

Rushing-in regrets happen when you should have taken more time to think about your actions or decisions before jumping forward. In a study, people's top coulda-woulda-shoulda was "Failure to seize the moment." But their second-biggest regret? "Rushing in too soon."[13]

It's easy to imagine your eighty-year-old self shouting at you, "Quit your job! Book that one-way plane ticket to Nepal! Life is short!" But it's not feasible to live every minute as if it's your last. And your eighty-year-old self would probably also be pretty grateful if you set her up with a healthy retirement savings account.

After reader Alyssa had her first child, she and her husband started house hunting. Their basement apartment felt too cramped for the three of them, and the paper-thin ceiling meant they could hear every step their upstairs neighbors took. There were also pests; one day, as Alyssa was reaching for a new diaper, a large spider dropped onto the changing table right next to her baby. It was time to go.

But finding a new home proved harder than expected. "Houses generally had offers the same day they were listed," Alyssa told us. When the couple finally found a house they loved, their offer was rejected. Devastated, they continued their search with a new sense of urgency. A few days later, another house in their price range popped up on the market, and they rushed to put in an offer. The house didn't have everything they wanted—the yard and kitchen were both small, the location wasn't ideal, and the split-level design meant there wasn't a lot of open space—but they figured they could make it work.

The moment they found out their offer was accepted, Alyssa felt the first twinge of doubt. "I was excited to be in a home but not so excited to be in the home we purchased," she admitted to us. Over time, as the drawbacks of the house became more and more apparent, Alyssa's regret grew.[14]

What to do about it: For rushing-in regrets, first try to understand the circumstances that led to your impatience. Ask yourself:

- How did I feel about the decision at the time I was making it?
- What was happening in my life that made me throw caution to the wind?

Based on your answers, think about some boundaries you can set (see page 99 for more advice on how to do this). For example, you might make a rule that you'll make big decisions only after sleeping on them for a night or two, or that you'll pause long enough to talk through options with a couple of trusted friends. Alyssa learned that "it's okay to want something and not have it yet." After spending six years in their first house, she and her husband are now looking to move again. "We're okay if the process takes significantly longer than it did the first time," Alyssa told us. "We want to wait until we find something that really works for us."

And the next time you're faced with a decision or find yourself in a similar spot, ask yourself a series of time-based questions:

- What would I regret most in a week?
- What about in a year?

- Ten years?
- Fifty years?

The goal of this exercise isn't to come up with perfect answers. After all, you don't really know who you're going to be in ten or fifty years. But you can stop and reflect on potential outcomes and then use what you learn to take a more informed, less spur-of-the-moment next step.

Dragging-out regrets are when you look back and think, "Why did I let that go on for so long?" or "Why did it take me so much time to do X or make a decision about X?" Maybe you stayed with an ex even though you knew that the relationship wasn't working, or you suffered in a place you hated for years before you decided it was finally time to leave.

Take reader Kia, who was married for ten years.[15] While the relationship looked perfect—she and her husband owned a beautiful house, had two dogs, and traveled often—he was extremely controlling. He commented often on what she ate, forced her to rely on him for her work visa, and put their bank accounts and benefits in his name. Kia knew their relationship wasn't healthy, but she was afraid of being alone and of having to find her own way, so she dragged out the decision to leave for years.

Getting a divorce was the hardest thing Kia has ever done. "I lost everything," she told us. "He had bank accounts canceled. Work visas canceled. Health insurance canceled."

But after a few months, Kia felt something besides devastated: she felt free. More than that, she had found ways to support herself and had reclaimed her self-confidence. "The end of my marriage taught me to rely on myself."

What to do about it: First, take a strengths-based approach to your self-talk. Instead of berating yourself with a statement like "I should have done X earlier," try saying, "I had the strength to do X, no matter how long it took me."

Then learn from past situations that you let drag on too long. Ask yourself:

- How did I know that what I was doing wasn't working?
- What kept me from acting sooner?

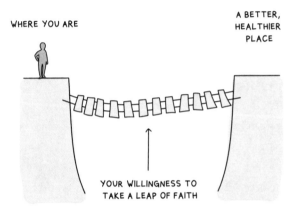

With dragging-out regret, there are a few common barriers to making a move:

- **Fear:** You're uncomfortable with the shift that the decision will trigger. It's useful to realize that most of the time, we don't fear change; we fear the uncertainty that comes with it (for more on this, see chapter 1).
- **Wanting more information:** You feel that you don't know enough to make a decision. Keep in mind that for some decisions, you will never have "enough" information, especially if you are a highly analytical person.
- **Waiting for the perfect moment:** You keep telling yourself the timing isn't quite right. Again, you may never feel that it's the right moment. Sometimes you just have to take a leap of faith.

Think back on your dragging-out regrets and see if you can identify a pattern—and look out for it in the future. For example, you can remind yourself, "I never feel that I have enough information, but I have learned that I tend to stay in negative situations for longer than I should. Is that what's happening now?"

A few other specific questions to ask yourself:

- What options do I have now?
- What's holding me back from acting this time? Are there ways to address those fears or factors?
- Is it possible to get back what I lost? If so, how?
- If not, how can I reframe the situation to get closure and agency for the future?

Since her divorce, Kia has worked hard to create a world that is entirely her own. She runs her own private practice, manages her finances, and is in a relationship with someone who celebrates her independence. She says her regret made her a stronger person. "Because of regret, I now make sure to speak my mind and I follow my instincts," Kia told us. "Because of regret, I am finally emerging."

Ignoring-your-instincts regrets are when you have an intuition about how to avoid a negative outcome or create a positive outcome but you disregard your gut. This frequently happens when you're making decisions with other people and you prioritize their reasoning, desires, or instincts over your own. People pleasers are most likely to feel this regret.

Mollie regrets that she didn't start trying to have children earlier. She wanted to start around age thirty. Her mom had two miscarriages while trying to conceive her younger sister, and Mollie knew how difficult that had been, both physically and emotionally. She had a strong intuition that she would have difficulty conceiving later in her thirties, a deep conviction that came from more than just looking at the fertility and age graphs.

Mollie's husband, Chris, wanted to wait longer to start trying. He grew up in a household where financial and career stability were an important part of being a good parent. And, working in a creative field, he kept feeling that he

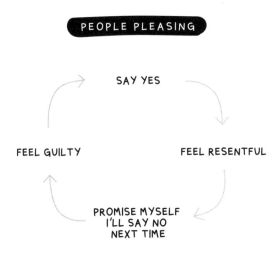

PEOPLE PLEASING

SAY YES

FEEL RESENTFUL

PROMISE MYSELF
I'LL SAY NO
NEXT TIME

FEEL GUILTY

was close to but not quite at a place where he could count on his paychecks being dependable. He worried that having a baby too soon would force him to choose between being the kind of parent he wanted to be and building a career that would provide for a family. He didn't think that Mollie was going to have difficulty conceiving, and they agreed to have another conversation when she was thirty-two. But when they did, Chris still didn't feel ready. Mollie was frustrated and complained to friends. They rolled their eyes and said, "Men are never ready." Mollie didn't want to pressure Chris or add to his job anxieties. But soon after that, she was injured, which then turned into chronic pain. So when Chris finally felt ready, Mollie didn't feel physically able to be pregnant.

What to do about it: First, give your gut credit for being correct. Then cut yourself some slack. It's not easy to convince yourself (or others) with an intuition-based argument. Then look back and think through answers to these questions:

- Who was I trying to please?
- What made me not act on my instincts?

- Why do I think I had that correct gut feeling?
- How can I listen to and act on these instincts in the future?

It can be useful to come up with a few ways to advocate for yourself and your intuition in the future. One phrase both Liz and Mollie have used successfully to communicate our feelings is "When you ____, I feel ____." You can also say something like "I feel strongly that ____. It's important to me that I explore this instinct, so I'd like to talk through reasons with you why I might feel this way."

Mollie regretted not communicating her feelings well to her husband. She regretted letting him convince her that there was no rush. But she learned how important it was to trust her instincts and to make sure that she and her husband fully understand where the other is coming from on subsequent big decisions.

Last, don't let your regret turn into resentment. Your instinct may have been spot-on, but holding on to resentment will make you and those around you unhappy.

To let go of her regret, Mollie had to reframe the decision she made with her husband. The story she tells herself now is that they made that decision together, and that if she had pressured him into having a child earlier, he would not have been ready. Or she would have gone through the same mental and physical health issues, but with a young child to care for. Mollie's story now is that her husband always wanted the best for both of them, but it took this crisis for him to understand how uncertain the future can be.

Self-sabotage regret happens after you do something that you consciously or unconsciously know is wrong in the moment because you're trying to protect yourself from another big, uncomfortable feeling. Maybe you cheat on a romantic partner because you're afraid of commitment, or you don't apply for a job to avoid the risk of rejection.

"For a long time, I found myself feeling insecure and anxious in social situations and often relied on alcohol to cope with those feelings," reader Alex told us.

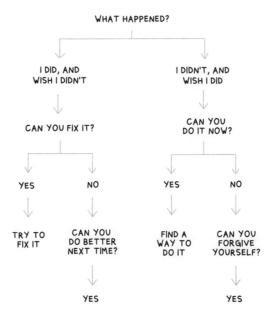

"After many mishaps and mistakes caused by drinking too much, I realized that I needed to stop worrying about whether or not I was fitting in and just be myself without the dependence on alcohol."[16]

What to do about it: Self-sabotage, more than any other type of regret, often requires deeper work that is easier to do with a therapist or support group. If you continually sabotage yourself, you most likely have some deep-seated beliefs about your value or your capacity to handle challenges. When we asked readers to share their top regrets, many included a version of "I wish I had loved myself more," because they'd made past decisions from a place of not feeling worthy. These notions can be changed, but they take long-term work that is best done in a supportive setting with trained experts at the helm.

Addiction can be a form of self-sabotage, although we will put an asterisk next to this statement, because addiction has a strong genetic component. As a member of Alcoholics Anonymous (AA) shared on his blog, "Alcoholism is a medical issue."[17] As with any form of addiction, people have less control over their decisions. The AA blogger explains that regrets stemming from addiction are less about moral choices than other types of regrets are. "Because of your (medical) condition, certain choices—or the ability to make better choices—just [weren't] available to you."

If your regrets stemming from self-sabotage (whether caused by addiction or not) involve hurting other people, you will need to make amends in order to move through the regret. Steps 8 through 10 in the AA program are as follows:

> **8.** Made a list of all persons we had harmed, and became willing to make amends to them all.
>
> **9.** Made direct amends to such people wherever possible, except when to do so would injure them or others.
>
> **10.** Continued to take personal inventory and when we were wrong promptly admitted it.[18]

(Note that we do not recommend skipping steps 1–7 in the AA program or dropping in on a twelve-step program without the guidance of others in recovery. We are sharing these steps to show that taking actions to heal from self-sabotage is critical to working through it.)

Take a careful look at your self-sabotage regrets, and for each one, ask yourself:

- Why did I make this decision?
- What was I trying to protect myself from?
- What do I wish I had done instead?

. . .

For all types of regret: Give yourself grace. Researchers at the University of California, Berkeley, found that people who accepted what had happened without endlessly beating themselves up about it were better able to harness regret as motivation to improve.

We also want to leave you with a few generally useful strategies for navigating moments of regret. Even if you've answered all the relevant questions we've suggested in this chapter, you'll likely still have flashes here and there where you find yourself fixated on what-ifs. Or you may experience a regret that doesn't fall neatly into one of the six buckets.

3. Remind yourself of what you gained

"'What might have been' is a pretty good definition of Hell," writes Rabbi Harold Kushner.[19]

When you're stuck in a regret rut, it's easy to spiral through all the things you should have done differently. The more vividly you imagine what could have happened, the stronger your emotional response will be. Psychologists call this *emotional amplification*.[20] (Movie directors use this technique to make you cry. When a character announces, "This is my last mission" or "I have a bad feeling about this," their death becomes all the more painful, because they almost made it out of harm's way.[21])

In other words, the more you indulge in fantasies of what might have been, the less likely you are to remember all the positives in your life.

When you find yourself overwhelmed by if-only scenarios, make it a point to nip your fantasizing in the bud by listing everything in your life that you're grateful for. "Whenever I have an I-wish-I-had thought," a workshop participant told us, "I ask myself: What memories and people would I have to give up for a 'maybe'? I usually change my mind."[22]

Researchers have shown that we're more able to feel better and move forward from regret when we reflect on these two prompts:[23]

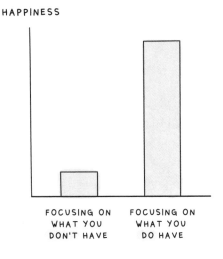

HAPPINESS

FOCUSING ON WHAT YOU DON'T HAVE

FOCUSING ON WHAT YOU DO HAVE

- Everything can be viewed from a different perspective
- There is positive value in every experience

In life, you miss out on some experiences to gain others. Author Charles Duhigg, speaking about his and his wife's decision to have children, admitted that he sometimes thinks about the books he might have written had he not had kids. "I would be just as happy without children," he shared. On the other hand, "I love my children. I love having children." He adds, "I am so glad we had [them] because I think it makes me a less selfish person. It makes me a better person."[24]

You can also tally up all the bad things you avoided. Say you picked a job that pays less but gives you a lot of flexibility. In moments when you regret your decision, vividly picture your free time swallowed up by work you don't enjoy.

4. Replace "should have" with "what if"

"Regret can be burned as fuel," writes author Augusten Burroughs. "To live in regret and change nothing else in your life is to miss the entire point."[25]

The next time you find yourself dwelling on a sentence that starts with "I should have . . . ," try swapping in the words "What if . . . ?" For example, if you think, "I should have been more confident in myself," ask yourself, "What if I acted with more confidence?" Then write out a few answers to your question.

Not every regret will perfectly map to this framework. Our friend Jackson once hit Send too soon on a half-baked salary negotiation email, which ended up costing him the job offer. Dwelling on the question "What if I hadn't prematurely hit Send?" only caused him to spiral further into regret. But looking at the bigger picture can still let you pull a useful what-if out of the worst situations. Jackson now asks himself, "What if I remove the sender's address before drafting an email? And what if I slow down a bit?"

Overcoming negative self-talk in the face of regret can feel like trying to get out of the parking lot after a Beyoncé concert. Try to surface the beliefs that you have surrounding your regrets by filling in these statements:

- I'm scared that because I did _____, _____ will never happen in the future.
- Since I used to _____, that means I'll always be a _____ person.
- I still blame myself for doing _____ in the past, and I'll never be able to let that go.
- I absolutely should have _____.

These are common regret-related thoughts—and they're signs that your self-reflection is turning self-destructive. Reread what you wrote, and reassess whether those statements are actually true (hint: they're not). Instead of telling yourself, "I absolutely should have advocated for myself," ask, "Why didn't I do that?" or

IMPORTANT REFRAMES

I SHOULD HAVE → WHAT IF

I MISSED MY CHANCE → WHAT CAN I DO TODAY?

I MADE A MISTAKE → NOW I KNOW WHAT NOT TO DO

"What if I started to advocate for myself more often?" Shifting to a more flexible mind-set will help you learn from your experiences and treat your past, present, and future self with more compassion.

5. Remember that regret will pass, or at least soften

While you may be experiencing regret now, know that someday you'll feel it less strongly. We often underestimate our ability to adapt to new circumstances and to make the most of what we have and where we are. "I used to feel like regret would last forever," a workshop participant told us. "But I've learned that it truly only lasts as long as I choose to dwell in it. I am being stubborn and holding on to what-ifs when I should move on and be grateful."

When Colin Jost asked his father if he regretted leaving the job he loved, his father responded, "Leaving was the best decision I ever made. Because eventually I started teaching, which meant I was home with you and your brother more after school. And I got to impact the lives of thousands of kids who came through my classroom, which is something I never knew was important to me until I went and did it."[26] The sting of intense regret fades and morphs with time, and in some cases, the "wrong decision" puts us on the path toward something even better.

. . .

No matter what path we take in life, we all will have moments when we experience some level of regret about the roads we chose not to travel. But done right, dwelling on what might have been can serve us. Crying over spilled milk enables us to understand where we've come from, how we got to where we are, and where we want to go. Just make sure to limit how long you linger on the past.

TAKEAWAYS

- A #NoRegrets life isn't possible; there are always trade-offs
- When you forecast potential regret, consider several time frames
- Allow yourself to grieve what wasn't
- Understand what type of regret you're feeling
- For hindsight and alternate-self regrets, try to nip romanticizing in the bud
- For other types of regret, learn from the past to improve your future
- Be gentle with yourself; we all make mistakes
- Remember that regret will soften over time

Conclusion

Big feelings can knock the wind out of us. We wrote this book to prove to ourselves that difficult emotions are not abnormal and that it is possible to emerge from them with newfound wisdom. Allowing ourselves to grieve the path we didn't walk can help us make more meaningful choices down the road. Tuning in to our strongest envy triggers can give us a clear sense of what we value. And even despair, when the light seems like it has been extinguished forever, can ultimately deepen our sense of self and our empathy for others.

At the same time, big feelings often feel traumatic and purposeless in the moment. We would rather not have to go through hard times than be forced to grow from them. But there is meaning to be found in the recovery process.

Even big feelings that don't seem helpful in the moment, like despair or perfectionism, can lead to something psychologists call *post-traumatic growth* (PTG). When we endure a period of great struggle or our core beliefs are challenged, we often emerge with an appreciation for the good things in life and a deeper sense of self. No one, for example, wants to go through horrific heartbreak, but sometimes a messy breakup can teach you what you want from your next partner and that there's a lot to love about yourself. Of course, we'd all probably pick not suffering over experiencing PTG. But it's helpful to know that even though it can feel like we're falling apart, we can emerge with something positive.

PTG affects people in the following specific ways:

1. They have a greater appreciation for life
2. They feel closer to their loved ones
3. They gain confidence in their ability to handle challenges
4. They experience a deeper sense of peace
5. They can see more possibilities for themselves[1]

In other words, our hardest moments can change us for the better. Experiencing big feelings is far from easy. But every time we're able to move through uncertainty or exhaustion or regret (even if it's just for a moment), we deepen our conviction that we can do it again. And again.

We (Liz and Mollie) have both changed since our previous book, *No Hard Feelings,* came out, and even over the course of writing the current book. Liz has learned to catch herself when she becomes too caught up in imagining catastrophic future scenarios and to be more accepting of her mood shifts. Mollie feels that she is less judgmental and rigid than she used to be. We both feel less alone in our struggles.

But we are not "cured" of life's challenges. Writing this book and working a full-time job made Liz's neck and arm pain flare up again. She and her husband are still mourning the death of his father while also supporting Liz's father as he struggles with health issues. Mollie is still in physical therapy for tendon pain in multiple parts of her body and had to get someone to help her type the majority of this book. She is still in therapy and on medication. We have both broken down in tears in the last month. Many times, we spoke to each other about the irony of writing a chapter on burnout while contending with it ourselves. As the poet Rainer Maria Rilke reminds us, "Do not think that *he* who tries to comfort you lives without effort amidst those calm and simple words that sometimes do you good. . . . Yet if it had been otherwise, he would never have been able to find these words."[2] In other words: anyone who is writing a book of advice is probably doing so because they've struggled with—and continue to struggle with—the same challenges.

We are both grateful for how much people were willing to open up to us for this book. We learned that our editor lost a parent as a young adult, and another editor lost a parent during COVID to alcoholism. These facts never came up in conversation when we were working together on *No Hard Feelings*. It can be scary to share these things with others, let alone to write a book about them and let the world in on your darkest times, but books have consoled us, and we can only try to pay it forward.

A therapist can be helpful with the process of exploring these difficult emotions (see "A Note on Therapy and Some Low-Cost and Free Options" on page 229). As reader Yalenka told us, "I sometimes joke that I need therapy to deal with those around me who don't go to therapy."

Even with therapy, it's important to keep in mind that all the tips we give are easier said than done. There is no shortcut for working through big feelings, and they won't ever fully go away. We all will feel stabs of regret from time to time, and we all will have days when life feels gloomy and hopeless. But over time, we can eventually get to a place where, even if a big feeling rears its head, it's okay.

We hope that this book, and the stories that others have let us share in it, provide you with some reassurance that even when things are not okay, *you* can still be okay.

Acknowledgments

Writing a book takes a village. Liz and Mollie would like to thank:

Leah Trouwborst, for believing in us a second time and being an engaged and energizing partner. Trish Daly, for jumping in midstream and expertly shepherding our vision to completion. Lisa DiMona, for endless support, always being on top of the trends, and helping us make sense out of our ideas. Julie Mosow, for best-in-class editing, bringing out our voices, and connecting on an emotional level. Laura Katz, for patient research and thoughtful suggestions.

The team at Writers House: Lauren Carsley, Maja Nikolic, Jessica Berger, and Chaim Lipskar for answering our endless questions and working on international rights.

The team at Penguin: Nina Rodriguez-Marty for the title. Brian Lemus for cover design. Ryan Boyle and Megan McCormack for the support. Stefanie Brody and Regina Andreoni for PR and marketing. Adrian Zackheim for being able to pitch our books back to us in a more elegant way than we pitched them originally.

All of the experts who gave us valuable time and ideas: Dr. Stefanie Tignor,

Dr. Molly Sands, Caribay Garcia, Cloe Shasha, Amy Bonsall, Dr. Emma Routhier, Dr. Thomas Greenspon, Tanya Geisler, and Rebecca Newkirk.

First readers: Grace Perry and Joanna Miller.

Authors who have championed us: Susan Cain, Adam Grant, Dan Pink, Malcolm Gladwell, and Laszlo Bock. Also to Panio Gianopoulos and the team at Next Big Idea Club for support.

Photographers: Nina Subin and Bonnie Rae Mills.

For the incredible individuals who were willing to share their stories with us: Priscilla, Yalenka, Leslie, Maike, Lisa, Naveed, Ellie, Meg, Nataly, Jay, Katja, Sarah, Yanelle, Elizabeth, Dave, Miriam, Amber Rae, Caribay, Susan, Jayna, Madhura, Allie, Daniela, Anna, Kristin, Eliza, Kia, Alex, Karla, Griffin, Rachel, Caroline, Gina, Kara, Joy, and everyone we promised not to name.

● ● ●

From Liz, thank you to:

Mollie: For being my ever-patient writing partner, for stepping in when I was down and out, for never attending parties on boats, and for prioritizing our friendship.

Mom and Dad: For always being my biggest champions, even when you're not quite sure what my job is or what the internet thing I'm showing you means. I love you.

Maxim: Thank you for "Vivify!," for letting me use Microsoft Word on your Dell, and for being the one person who can unfailingly make my day go from bad to the best.

Everyone who helped make this book happen, whether that meant reviewing drafts, opening up about your experiences, or just making me laugh when I needed it: Marina A., Carmen A., Vivek A., B. A., Erica A., Nick D., Susan E., Jay F., Susan F., Wenche F., Caitlin G., Griffin G., Caribay G., Anne H., Dennis H., Becca J., Hee-Sun K., Carly K., Cori L., Emily M., Jason N., Emily N., Josh R., the Reeds, Molly S., Kris S., Stefanie T., Erik T., Christine T., Logan U., and Hannah Y.

Everyone who follows @lizandmollie on social media: I cannot say enough how much all the comments and messages mean to me. One of the highlights of my life is getting to connect with so many of you, especially over the things that often feel hard to talk about.

And finally, to my past and present colleagues: Andy Wong, you continue to be my guiding light. Reigan and everyone at Humu, thank you for supporting me in taking the time I needed to bring this book into the world.

. . .

From Mollie, thank you to:

Liz: For agreeing to take on a second book even after we agreed we would never do this to ourselves again. Seeing your illustrations never stops being my favorite part. Also, for being the best listener and caring friend.

My family: For love and support during the ups and downs, especially Laura, Kate, David, Jackie, Sarah, Jenny, and the Duffys. Thank you to Judy for sharing wisdom and hope from your own life.

Those who helped with research and writing: Kainoa Cunningham, Sadé Harper, Meta Daniel, Andrea Vega, and Reilly Blevins.

Friends who check in, and who can talk about and listen to hard things: Julia B. for daily texts, Annie, Julia M., Sophie, Emily, Skylar, Hayley, Hannah, Christine, Danielle, Lillie, Nse, Alice K., Caitlin, Julia S., Meryl, and Katie O.

All of my current and past colleagues and clients: For inspiration and support.

Everyone who helped along my healing journey: Lindsay Brunner, Patrick O'Rourke, Jared Vagy (PTs extraordinaire), Sharon Rafferty (therapist extraordinaire), Gina P., Meg L., Rachel K., Maurine K., Susan M., and Rabbi Susan Goldberg and the Nefesh Los Angeles community.

And finally to Chris: My funny, kind-hearted, creative, and captivating husband. Thank you for your unending support, patience, and love. It means the world to me. I like you and I love you.

Big Feelings Assessments

Based on the Maslach Burnout Inventory

Step 1. Indicate how frequently the following statements apply to you:

1 = Never
2 = At least a few times a year
3 = At least once a month
4 = Several times a month
5 = Once a week
6 = Several times a week
7 = Every day

1. I feel emotionally exhausted because of my work
   Never 1 — 2 — 3 — 4 — 5 — 6 — 7 *Every day*

2. I feel worn out at the end of a workday

   Never 1 — 2 — 3 — 4 — 5 — 6 — 7 *Every day*

3. I feel tired as soon as I get up in the morning and see a new workday stretched out in front of me

   Never 1 — 2 — 3 — 4 — 5 — 6 — 7 *Every day*

4. I can easily understand the actions of my colleagues/supervisors

   Never 1 — 2 — 3 — 4 — 5 — 6 — 7 *Every day*

5. I get the feeling that I treat some clients/colleagues impersonally, as if they were objects

   Never 1 — 2 — 3 — 4 — 5 — 6 — 7 *Every day*

6. Working and collaborating with people is stressful for me

   Never 1 — 2 — 3 — 4 — 5 — 6 — 7 *Every day*

7. I deal with other people's problems successfully

   Never 1 — 2 — 3 — 4 — 5 — 6 — 7 *Every day*

8. I feel burned out because of my work

   Never 1 — 2 — 3 — 4 — 5 — 6 — 7 *Every day*

9. I feel that I influence other people positively through my work

   Never 1 — 2 — 3 — 4 — 5 — 6 — 7 *Every day*

10. I have become more callous toward people since I started this job

    Never 1 — 2 — 3 — 4 — 5 — 6 — 7 *Every day*

11. I'm afraid that my work makes me emotionally distant

    Never 1 — 2 — 3 — 4 — 5 — 6 — 7 *Every day*

12. I feel full of energy

    Never 1 — 2 — 3 — 4 — 5 — 6 — 7 *Every day*

13. I feel frustrated by my work

    Never 1 — 2 — 3 — 4 — 5 — 6 — 7 *Every day*

14. I get the feeling that I work too hard

    Never 1 — 2 — 3 — 4 — 5 — 6 — 7 *Every day*

15. I'm not really interested in what is going on with many of my colleagues

    Never 1 — 2 — 3 — 4 — 5 — 6 — 7 *Every day*

16. Being in direct contact with people at work is stressful

Never 1 — 2 — 3 — 4 — 5 — 6 — 7 Every day

17. I find it easy to build a relaxed atmosphere in my work environment

Never 1 — 2 — 3 — 4 — 5 — 6 — 7 Every day

18. I feel stimulated when I work closely with my colleagues

Never 1 — 2 — 3 — 4 — 5 — 6 — 7 Every day

19. I have achieved many rewarding objectives in my work

Never 1 — 2 — 3 — 4 — 5 — 6 — 7 Every day

20. I feel as if I'm at my wits' end

Never 1 — 2 — 3 — 4 — 5 — 6 — 7 Every day

21. In my work, I am very relaxed when dealing with emotional problems

Never 1 — 2 — 3 — 4 — 5 — 6 — 7 Every day

22. I have the feeling that my colleagues blame me for some of their problems

Never 1 — 2 — 3 — 4 — 5 — 6 — 7 Every day

Step 2. Add together your answers to find your scores:

Overall score for **exhaustion:**

Add up your scores from questions 1, 2, 3, 6, 8, 13, 14, 16, 20

≤ 20	21–42	≥ 43
Low degree	Moderate degree	High degree
		of exhaustion

Overall score for **cynicism:**

Add up your scores from questions 5, 10, 11, 15, 22

≤ 11	12–23	≥ 24
Low degree	Moderate degree	High degree
		of cynicism

Overall score for *ineffectiveness:*

Add up your scores from questions 4, 7, 9, 12, 17, 18, 19, 21

≥ 38	37–19	≤ 18
Low degree	Moderate degree	High degree
		of ineffectiveness

Step 3. Use your scores from Step 2 to find your Burnout Profile Assessment:

- **Engaged:** Low to moderate degree of **exhaustion, cynicism,** and **ineffectiveness**
  - You're doing pretty well. Or at least okay.
  - **Your main opportunity:** *Monitor what situations cause you to inch toward burnout, and actively set boundaries.*
- **Overextended:** High degree of **exhaustion**
  - Everything feels overwhelming, and you're overworked. Feeling overextended is often the result of having too much work or being in an always-on work culture. But it can also happen when you have taken on too many side projects or have time-consuming health issues or family obligations.
  - **Your main opportunity:** *Get comfortable living life at 80 percent. Reduce the number of hours you work (whether the work is for your day job or other obligations). Learn to draw—and respect—your own lines.*
- **Disengaged:** High degree of **cynicism**
  - You don't feel connected to your colleagues, and you lack empathy for those around you. We often become disengaged when we're overdoing it, or when we no longer feel that what we do matters.
  - **Your main opportunity:** *Find small ways to connect or reconnect with colleagues.*

- **Ineffective:** High degree of **ineffectiveness**
  - You feel incompetent and unproductive. You may actually be effective at your job, but your perception is that you are ineffective.
  - **Your main opportunity:** *Get clear on what you value, and shift your work to align with those values.*
- **Burned out:** High degree of **exhaustion, cynicism,** and **ineffectiveness**
  - You are beyond tired—you are discouraged and alienated.
  - **Your main opportunity:** *Detach your worth from what you do, and make time for "garbage time."*

PERFECTIONISM ASSESSMENT

Are you a healthy striver or a perfectionist?

Step 1. Indicate where you fall on the scale between the two options:

1. You've got a "just for fun" project to work on today. How do you feel about it?
   Invigorated and excited 1 — 2 — 3 — 4 — 5 — 6 — 7 Terrified: Will the final product be good enough?

2. How often do you miss deadlines because you're anxious about whether your work is good enough?
   Never 1 — 2 — 3 — 4 — 5 — 6 — 7 Often

3. How often do you think, "I'll feel accomplished or worthy of praise once I _____"?
   Never 1 — 2 — 3 — 4 — 5 — 6 — 7 Often

4. When you step away from work for the day, you:

Mentally move on 1 — 2 — 3 — 4 — 5 — 6 — 7 *Ruminate over the day's faults and remaining to-dos*

5. Without external validation, you think, "My hard work paid off. That's pretty good!"

Very often 1 — 2 — 3 — 4 — 5 — 6 — 7 *Never*

6. When you receive external validation, which are you more likely to think?

I'm glad they see my hard work! 1 — 2 — 3 — 4 — 5 — 6 — 7 *How are they missing all the flaws?*

7. You're extremely tired. Which are you more likely to do?

Hit the brakes 1 — 2 — 3 — 4 — 5 — 6 — 7 *Use anxiety as fuel and keep moving*

8. You overslept and missed your Saturday morning exercise class. How do you feel about your day?

Fine, I can exercise later 1 — 2 — 3 — 4 — 5 — 6 — 7 *It's ruined. Why am I always so unproductive?*

9. You said you'd bring dessert to a potluck with friends. How do you feel about it?

Happy to contribute 1 — 2 — 3 — 4 — 5 — 6 — 7 *STRESSED!! I'm afraid they'll hate it*

Step 2. Add together your answers to find your score and perfectionism tendency:

- **20 or less: You're a healthy striver.**
  - When you care about a project, it's good motivation for you to work hard, get it done on time, and feel proud of it when you're finished.

- **Your main opportunity:** *Monitor what situations cause you to inch into some perfectionist tendencies (we all do!), and mitigate those triggers.*

- **21–42: You have some perfectionistic tendencies.**
  - These may show up when you're really invested in a project, or in some realms of your life more than others (for example, you're a perfectionist at work but not in social situations).
  - **Your main opportunity:** *Try using a perfectionism journal. Identify the moments when you feel your perfectionist doubts starting to creep in, and compare them with the moments of feeling satisfied with your efforts. What's the difference? Is a particular person or type of activity triggering your perfectionism/feelings of inadequacy? How can you avoid or mitigate those triggers?*

- **43 or more: You're a full-blown perfectionist.**
  - Your mantra seems to be "If I'm going to do it, I'm going to do it perfectly." It guides you whether or not you really care about a project, and it shows up in many areas of your life, whether personal or work-related.
  - **Your main opportunity:** *To perfectionists, "good enough" doesn't feel good enough. But putting 110 percent into all your projects will lead to burnout. Try looking at the section on values in chapter 4. Which of your current activities or tasks fall outside your core values? Can you let go of "perfect" for one or more of them?*

ANGER EXPRESSION TENDENCY

This is a modified assessment based on the State-Trait Anger Expression Inventory-2 (STAXI-2), a test used by therapists to assess various aspects of a person's anger and how those relate to psychological and medical conditions.

Four of those aspects are traits that relate to anger expression, and they are considered to be relatively independent of one another.

Step 1. Indicate how frequently the following statements apply to you:

1. I stop myself from losing my temper
   Frequently 1 — 2 — 3 — 4 — 5 — 6 — 7 *Rarely*
2. I do not express my anger
   Frequently 1 — 2 — 3 — 4 — 5 — 6 — 7 *Rarely*
3. When angry, I say mean or nasty things
   Frequently 1 — 2 — 3 — 4 — 5 — 6 — 7 *Rarely*
4. When angry, I try to understand and get in touch with what triggered the anger
   Frequently 1 — 2 — 3 — 4 — 5 — 6 — 7 *Rarely*
5. If annoyed, I share how I feel
   Frequently 1 — 2 — 3 — 4 — 5 — 6 — 7 *Rarely*
6. When angry, I try to calm down
   Frequently 1 — 2 — 3 — 4 — 5 — 6 — 7 *Rarely*
7. I lose my temper
   Frequently 1 — 2 — 3 — 4 — 5 — 6 — 7 *Rarely*
8. I control my angry feelings
   Frequently 1 — 2 — 3 — 4 — 5 — 6 — 7 *Rarely*
9. I try to soothe my angry feelings
   Frequently 1 — 2 — 3 — 4 — 5 — 6 — 7 *Rarely*
10. Instead of getting angry, I feel sad or depressed
    Frequently 1 — 2 — 3 — 4 — 5 — 6 — 7 *Rarely*
11. I argue with others
    Frequently 1 — 2 — 3 — 4 — 5 — 6 — 7 *Rarely*

12. When angry, I pause and recognize that I am angry

    Frequently 1 — 2 — 3 — 4 — 5 — 6 — 7 *Rarely*

13. I am uncomfortable with conflict

    Frequently 1 — 2 — 3 — 4 — 5 — 6 — 7 *Rarely*

14. I am more irritated than other people realize

    Frequently 1 — 2 — 3 — 4 — 5 — 6 — 7 *Rarely*

15. When angry, I do something relaxing to calm down

    Frequently 1 — 2 — 3 — 4 — 5 — 6 — 7 *Rarely*

16. I feel defensive when people ask if I'm angry

    Frequently 1 — 2 — 3 — 4 — 5 — 6 — 7 *Rarely*

17. I do things like slam doors

    Frequently 1 — 2 — 3 — 4 — 5 — 6 — 7 *Rarely*

18. When angry, I try to be patient with myself and others

    Frequently 1 — 2 — 3 — 4 — 5 — 6 — 7 *Rarely*

19. I express my anger

    Frequently 1 — 2 — 3 — 4 — 5 — 6 — 7 *Rarely*

20. I tend to harbor grudges

    Frequently 1 — 2 — 3 — 4 — 5 — 6 — 7 *Rarely*

21. I pout or sulk

    Frequently 1 — 2 — 3 — 4 — 5 — 6 — 7 *Rarely*

22. I feel guilty or ashamed when I'm angry

    Frequently 1 — 2 — 3 — 4 — 5 — 6 — 7 *Rarely*

23. I am known as someone who keeps my cool under pressure

    Frequently 1 — 2 — 3 — 4 — 5 — 6 — 7 *Rarely*

24. I shut down or isolate from people when I'm upset

    Frequently 1 — 2 — 3 — 4 — 5 — 6 — 7 *Rarely*

25. I make sarcastic remarks to others

    Frequently 1 — 2 — 3 — 4 — 5 — 6 — 7 *Rarely*

26. I become sullen

    Frequently 1 — 2 — 3 — 4 — 5 — 6 — 7 *Rarely*

27. I try to be tolerant and understanding

    Frequently 1 — 2 — 3 — 4 — 5 — 6 — 7 *Rarely*

28. I can be passive-aggressive in expressing anger

    Frequently 1 — 2 — 3 — 4 — 5 — 6 — 7 *Rarely*

29. I ignore things that bother or upset me rather than addressing them

    Frequently 1 — 2 — 3 — 4 — 5 — 6 — 7 *Rarely*

30. I am passive when expressing anger

    Frequently 1 — 2 — 3 — 4 — 5 — 6 — 7 *Rarely*

31. I feel bitter, envious, or resentful

    Frequently 1 — 2 — 3 — 4 — 5 — 6 — 7 *Rarely*

32. I am aggressive in the way I express my anger

    Frequently 1 — 2 — 3 — 4 — 5 — 6 — 7 *Rarely*

33. I feel that expressing anger is unpleasant

    Frequently 1 — 2 — 3 — 4 — 5 — 6 — 7 *Rarely*

Step 2. Add together your answers to find your scores and your anger expression tendencies:

Anger controller:

Add up your scores from questions 1, 2, 8, 13, 23, 30, 33

≤ 16	17–32	≥ 33
Low degree	Moderate degree	High degree
		of anger control

- **For moderate to high degree scores:** You have a tendency to control how you express your anger. You monitor yourself to avoid expressing uncontrolled anger. You may experience anger but not be completely in tune with the need behind it. So you are not able to understand and resolve the cause of the anger.
- **Your main opportunity:** *Get comfortable with your own anger. Experiencing it should not cause you discomfort. Focus on consciously recognizing your anger so you can address the root cause.*

Anger transformer:

Add up your scores from questions 4, 6, 9, 12, 15, 18, 27

≤ 16	17–32	≥ 33
Low degree	Moderate degree	High degree
		of anger transformation

- **For moderate to high degree scores:** When you are feeling angry, you try to resolve the anger by recognizing it and understanding the deeper need. You use techniques like meditating, breath work, and patience to help work through the anger in a productive way rather than suppressing it. You understand that anger can be clarifying and healthy (when not projected outward onto others or inward toward yourself).

- **Your main opportunity:** *Keep doing what you are doing. Notice when you slip into less-healthy ways of expressing your anger, and what the triggers are.*

Anger projector:

Add up your scores from questions 3, 5, 7, 11, 17, 19, 21, 25, 32

≤ 20	21–42	≥ 43
Low degree	Moderate degree	High degree
		of anger projection

- **For moderate to high degree scores:** You frequently express your anger in an aggressive way, toward either other people or objects. You may express your anger physically (for example, slamming doors) or verbally (insults, profanity, sarcasm).

- **Your main opportunity:** *Your goal should be not to repress your anger but, instead, to express it in a healthier way. One way to express anger creatively is through writing (journaling, writing letters you will never send) or movement (dancing, running, yoga).*

Work on accepting your anger and developing ways to let it out in a way that's less toxic to those around you.

Anger suppressor:

Add up your scores from questions 10, 14, 16, 20, 22, 24, 26, 28, 29, 31

≤ 19	20–39	≥ 39
Low degree	Moderate degree	High degree
		of anger suppression

- **For moderate to high degree scores:** You suppress your anger. In some cases, feeling angry is so uncomfortable that instead of freely feeling it, you feel a different emotion instead, like sadness or guilt. You may have a tendency to blame yourself for the situation that was the basis for your anger, even though you are not to blame. When anger is suppressed, it tends to lead to anxiety and depression. Anger suppression is also associated with hypertension and high blood pressure.

- **Your main opportunity:** *Focus on freely expressing your anger in a productive way that does not dump onto other people. Open expression allows you to work through the emotion to resolve it in a conscious way.*

UNCERTAINTY TOLERANCE ASSESSMENT

This is a modified assessment based on the Intolerance of Uncertainty Scale (IUS), which measures responses to uncertainty, ambiguous situations, and the future.

Step 1. Indicate where you fall on the scale between the two options:

1. Unforeseen events upset me greatly

   Doesn't sound like me 1 — 2 — 3 — 4 — 5 — 6 — 7 *Sounds exactly like me*

2. It frustrates me not having all the information I need

    Doesn't sound like me 1 — 2 — 3 — 4 — 5 — 6 — 7 *Sounds exactly like me*

3. Uncertainty keeps me from living a full life

    Doesn't sound like me 1 — 2 — 3 — 4 — 5 — 6 — 7 *Sounds exactly like me*

4. One should always look ahead so as to avoid surprises

    Doesn't sound like me 1 — 2 — 3 — 4 — 5 — 6 — 7 *Sounds exactly like me*

5. A small unforeseen event can spoil everything, even with the best of planning

    Doesn't sound like me 1 — 2 — 3 — 4 — 5 — 6 — 7 *Sounds exactly like me*

6. When it's time to act, uncertainty paralyzes me

    Doesn't sound like me 1 — 2 — 3 — 4 — 5 — 6 — 7 *Sounds exactly like me*

7. When I am uncertain, I can't function very well

    Doesn't sound like me 1 — 2 — 3 — 4 — 5 — 6 — 7 *Sounds exactly like me*

8. I always want to know what the future has in store for me

    Doesn't sound like me 1 — 2 — 3 — 4 — 5 — 6 — 7 *Sounds exactly like me*

9. I can't stand being taken by surprise

    Doesn't sound like me 1 — 2 — 3 — 4 — 5 — 6 — 7 *Sounds exactly like me*

10. The smallest doubt can stop me from acting

    Doesn't sound like me 1 — 2 — 3 — 4 — 5 — 6 — 7 *Sounds exactly like me*

11. I should be able to organize everything in advance

    Doesn't sound like me 1 — 2 — 3 — 4 — 5 — 6 — 7 *Sounds exactly like me*

12. I must get away from all uncertain situations

    Doesn't sound like me 1 — 2 — 3 — 4 — 5 — 6 — 7 *Sounds exactly like me*

Step 2. Add together your answers to find your scores and your uncertainty tolerance assessment:

- **28 or less: You are an uncertainty seeker.**
  - Uncertain situations don't stress you out much. In fact, you may thrive in fast-changing environments.

- **Your main opportunity:** *Keep an eye out, as your uncertainty tolerance may change over time. But for the moment, you might find yourself happiest with a professional or personal life that involves a lot of ebb and flow. If you feel understimulated, is there a way you can incorporate more variation into work or other parts of your life? If so, it may jump-start your joie de vivre!*

- **29–56: You are an uncertainty balancer.**
  - Your tolerance for uncertain situations may vary, depending on the realm of your life (personal versus professional) or other factors, like how much sleep you're getting.

  - **Your main opportunity:** *If you feel like your work or personal life is stretching your uncertainty tolerance (and possibly your mental health), see if there are ways that you can incorporate more regularity into your day. For specific ideas, check out the sidebar on* **"Small ways to ground yourself when everything is up in the air"** *in chapter 1. On the other hand, if you're feeling understimulated in some part of your life, see if there are ways that you can incorporate more variation into your day, week, or year.*

- **57 or more: You are an uncertainty avoider.**
  - You're often attuned to the uncertainty of life. If you have a high-uncertainty job (e.g., your projects are constantly shifting, or you're moving around a lot), this may put extra strain on your mental health.

  - **Your main opportunity:** *For short-term help, consider* **"Small ways to ground yourself when everything is up in the air" in chapter 1.** *However, you may need to make some larger, long-term changes to better honor your need for more certainty. This may clash with visions you've had for yourself;* **Myth #2 in chapter 7** *may help you think more deeply about these issues. But in general, the better your mental health, the better equipped you'll be to handle unavoidable uncertainty.*

List of General Resources

A NOTE ON THERAPY AND SOME LOW-COST AND FREE OPTIONS

As we've said, therapy can be incredibly transformative, but in many cases, it takes months (or years) of weekly sessions to truly untangle trauma or harmful patterns of thinking. Unfortunately, this means that therapy costs can add up, particularly if your insurance plan has a high deductible or won't pay for a specific type of therapist. For example, if you are struggling with post-traumatic stress disorder or disordered eating/an eating disorder, you may want to see someone who specializes in those issues.

If you are having trouble finding a therapist who suits your individual needs and is within your budget, here are a few lower-cost options to explore.

- Some therapists charge on a sliding scale, usually between $75 and $160 per session, depending on what their clients can afford to pay. For help finding such therapists, check out the directories at **goodtherapy.org** and the *Psychology Today* website.

- The nonprofit **Open Path Collective** has a network of about fourteen thousand therapists with different specialties. After an initial, one-time membership fee of $60, they provide counseling online or in person for $30 to $80 a session.
- A good resource for free or lowest-cost options is local clinics, where mental health services are often provided by students (for example, those studying psychotherapy or social work) overseen by experienced professionals. As a result, they can often provide a wide range of services at no or extremely low cost. To find clinics:
  - Contact the **National Alliance on Mental Illness (NAMI) HelpLine** (info@nami.org; 800-950-6264) for referrals.
  - Go to **mentalhealth.gov** or the website of the Substance Abuse and Mental Health Services Administration, **https://findtreatment.samhsa.gov/locator**. With the latter, you can check boxes to search for facilities with payment assistance or sliding-scale options.
  - Ask **your primary health care provider** about options in your area.

It's also best if you feel a sense of trust and connection with your therapist. If you are able, you may want to meet with a few different therapists at first, to see who you click with. Just let them know before or during an initial meeting that you are still checking out a few different therapy options.

GENERAL BOOKS THAT MAY BE HELPFUL WHEN YOU'RE MOVING THROUGH A BIG FEELING

- *The Poetry Remedy: Prescriptions for the Heart, Mind, and Soul* by William Sieghart
- *How Lovely the Ruins: Inspirational Poems and Words for Difficult Times*, edited by Annie Chagnot and Emi Ikkanda

- *Everything Happens for a Reason: And Other Lies I've Loved* by Kate Bowler
- *We Are the Luckiest: The Surprising Magic of a Sober Life* by Laura McKowen
- *Maybe You Should Talk to Someone: A Therapist, Her Therapist, and Our Lives Revealed* by Lori Gottlieb
- *When Bad Things Happen to Good People* by Harold S. Kushner
- *Brave Enough* by Cheryl Strayed
- *Good Poems for Hard Times*, edited by Garrison Keillor
- *Stitches: A Handbook on Meaning, Hope and Repair* by Anne Lamott
- *Radical Acceptance: Embracing Your Life with the Heart of a Buddha* by Tara Brach
- *First, We Make the Beast Beautiful: A New Journey through Anxiety* by Sarah Wilson
- *Why Buddhism Is True: The Science and Philosophy of Meditation and Enlightenment* by Robert Wright
- *Going to Pieces without Falling Apart: A Buddhist Perspective on Wholeness* by Mark Epstein
- *Minor Feelings: An Asian American Reckoning* by Cathy Park Hong

List of Resources by Chapter

CHAPTER 1: UNCERTAINTY
LIST OF FAVORITE GUIDED MEDITATIONS

- Insight Timer app (free):
  - Tara Brach: "Breath and Awareness," "A Pause for Presence," "Vipassana (Basic) Meditation"
  - Sarah Blondin: "You Are Allowed," "Learning to Surrender," "Accepting Change"
  - Judson Brewer: "Working with Stress," "Body Scan for When You Only Have a Few Minutes"
  - Annemaree Rowley: "Letting Go Meditation," "Pause"
  - Jack Kornfield: "Breathing Meditation," "How to Transform Any Hard Situation"
  - Wim Hof: "Invigorating Breathing Exercise"
  - Mary Maddux: "Guided Meditation for Patience"
  - Thich Nhat Hanh: "Mindful Breathing," "How Do We Deal with Regrets?"

- Ten Percent Happier app (a few free tracks but mostly membership based):
  - Sharon Salzberg: "Feeling the Breath," "Balance"
  - Joseph Goldstein: "Fear," "Mindfulness Meditation"
  - Jon Kabat-Zinn: "Attending to Awareness"
- Calm (a few free tracks but mostly membership based):
  - Jeff Warren: "How to Meditate Series," "Daily Trip Highlights"
  - Elisha Goldstein: "Anxiety Release"
  - Tara Brach: "Relaxed Open-hearted Presence"
  - Tamara Levitt: "Emotions Series"
  - Oren Jay Sofer: "7 Days of Soothing Pain"

CHAPTER 3: ANGER
RESOURCES ON ANGER

- *Rage Becomes Her: The Power of Women's Anger* by Soraya Chemaly
- *This Is How: Surviving What You Think You Can't* by Augusten Burroughs
- *Angry White Men: American Masculinity at the End of an Era* by Michael Kimmel
- *Good and Mad: The Revolutionary Power of Women's Anger* by Rebecca Traister
- *The Anger Gap: How Race Shapes Emotion in Politics* by Davin L. Phoenix
- *The End of Anger: A New Generation's Take on Race and Rage* by Ellis Cose
- *Sister Outsider: Essays and Speeches* by Audre Lorde

CHAPTER 4: BURNOUT
LIST OF VALUES (SOURCE: JAMES CLEAR)

- Achievement
- Adventure
- Authenticity
- Authority
- Autonomy
- Balance

- Beauty
- Boldness
- Challenge
- Citizenship
- Community
- Compassion
- Competency
- Contribution
- Creativity
- Curiosity
- Determination
- Fairness
- Faith
- Fame
- Friendship
- Fun
- Growth
- Happiness
- Honesty
- Humor
- Influence
- Inner Harmony
- Justice
- Kindness
- Knowledge
- Leadership
- Learning
- Love
- Loyalty
- Meaningful Work
- Openness
- Optimism
- Peace
- Pleasure
- Poise
- Popularity
- Recognition
- Religion
- Reputation
- Respect
- Responsibility
- Security
- Self-respect
- Service
- Spirituality
- Stability
- Status
- Success
- Trustworthiness
- Wealth
- Wisdom

CHAPTER 5: PERFECTIONISM

RESOURCES ON SHAME AND GUILT

- *I Thought It Was Just Me (but It Isn't): Making the Journey from "What Will People Think?" to "I Am Enough"* by Brené Brown
- *The Gifts of Imperfection: Let Go of Who You Think You're Supposed to Be and Embrace Who You Are* by Brené Brown
- *The Body Keeps the Score: Brain, Mind, and Body in the Healing of Trauma* by Bessel van der Kolk
- "What's the Difference Between Guilt and Shame?" TED Talk by June Tangney

CHAPTER 6: DESPAIR
RESOURCES ON SUICIDE

- National Suicide Prevention Lifeline, 800-273-8255 (available 24/7; English, Spanish)
- To Write Love on Her Arms, twloha.com/find-help
- The Trevor Project, thetrevorproject.org
- *So Much I Want to Tell You: Letters to My Little Sister* by Anna Akana
- *If You Feel Too Much: Thoughts on Things Found and Lost and Hoped For* by Jamie Tworkowski
- *Boy Meets Depression: Or Life Sucks and Then You ~~Die~~ Live* by Kevin Breel
- *You Will Get Through This Night* by Daniel Howell

RESOURCES ON DESPAIR

- *When Things Fall Apart: Heart Advice for Difficult Times* by Pema Chödrön
- *On Being* (podcast) episode, "The Soul in Depression"
- *The Noonday Demon: An Atlas of Depression* by Andrew Solomon
- *Faith: Trusting Your Own Deepest Experience* by Sharon Salzberg
- *Full Catastrophe Living: Using the Wisdom of Your Body and Mind to Face Stress, Pain, and Illness* by Jon Kabat-Zinn

RESOURCES ON GRIEF

- *Resilient Grieving: Finding Strength and Embracing Life after a Loss That Changes Everything* by Lucy Hone
- *Option B: Facing Adversity, Building Resilience, and Finding Joy* by Sheryl Sandberg and Adam Grant

- *The Beauty of What Remains: How Our Greatest Fear Becomes Our Greatest Gift* by Steve Leder
- *Finding Meaning: The Sixth Stage of Grief* by David Kessler

RESOURCES ON CHRONIC PAIN

- *The Lady's Handbook for Her Mysterious Illness: A Memoir* by Sarah Ramey
- *Invisible: How Young Women with Serious Health Issues Navigate Work, Relationships, and the Pressure to Seem Just Fine* by Michele Lent Hirsch
- *The Anatomy of Hope: How People Prevail in the Face of Illness* by Jerome Groopman
- *Disability Visibility: First-Person Stories from the Twenty-First Century* by Alice Wong
- *More Beautiful Than Before: How Suffering Transforms Us* by Steve Leder

Notes

INTRODUCTION

1. Valerie Strauss, "Feeling Bad about Feeling Bad Can Make You Feel Really, Really Bad. New Research Really Says This," *The Washington Post*, August 10, 2017, www.washingtonpost.com /news/answer-sheet/wp/2017/08/10/feeling-bad-about-feeling-bad-can-make-you-feel-really -really-bad-new-research-really-says-this.
2. Ruth Whippman, *America the Anxious* (New York: St. Martin's Press, 2016), 201.
3. James Coyne, "Positive Psychology Is Mainly for Rich White People," *Coyne of the Realm*, August 23, 2013, www.coyneoftherealm.com/2013/08/21/positive-psychology-is-mainly-for -rich-white-people.
4. Erin Petrun, "Happy Week: Positive Psychology," CBS News, September 14, 2009, www.cbs news.com/news/happy-week-positive-psychology.

CHAPTER 1: UNCERTAINTY

1. Adam Tooze, quoted in Neil Irwin, "It's the End of the World Economy as We Know It," *The New York Times*, April 16, 2020, www.nytimes.com/2020/04/16/upshot/world-economy -restructuring-coronavirus.html.
2. Guy Trebay, videos by Isak Tiner, "Awake at 3 A.M.? We Are Too," *The New York Times*, October 30, 2020, www.nytimes.com/2020/10/30/style/insomnia-why-am-i-waking-up-at-3-am .html.
3. Annie Lowrey, "Millennials Don't Stand a Chance," *The Atlantic*, April 13, 2020, www.the atlantic.com/ideas/archive/2020/04/millennials-are-new-lost-generation/609832.

4. Robert M. Sapolsky, *Why Zebras Don't Get Ulcers* (New York: W. H. Freeman, 1994).

5. Julie Beck, "How Uncertainty Fuels Anxiety," *The Atlantic*, March 18, 2015, www.theatlantic .com/health/archive/2015/03/how-uncertainty-fuels-anxiety/388066.

6. Google Trends search: unprecedented, https://trends.google.com/trends/explore?date=today %205-y&q=unprecedented.

7. Alexandra Ossola, "Why Are Humans So Bad at Predicting the Future?," *Quartz*, November 20, 2019, https://qz.com/1752106/why-are-humans-so-bad-at-predicting-the-future.

8. Pema Chödrön, *Comfortable with Uncertainty: 108 Teachings on Cultivating Fearlessness and Compassion* (Boulder, CO: Shambhala, 2018), 5.

9. Yuval Rottenstreich and Christopher K. Hsee, "Money, Kisses, and Electric Shocks: On the Affective Psychology of Risk," *Psychological Science* 12, no. 3 (2001): 185–90, https://doi.org /10.1111/1467-9280.00334.

10. Manisha Aggarwal-Schifellite and Juan Siliezar, "3 Takes on Dealing with Uncertainty," *Harvard Gazette*, July 10, 2020, https://news.harvard.edu/gazette/story/2020/07/3-takes-on-dealing -with-uncertainty.

11. Marc Lewis, "Why We're Hardwired to Hate Uncertainty," *The Guardian*, April 8, 2016, www .theguardian.com/commentisfree/2016/apr/04/uncertainty-stressful-research-neuroscience.

12. Archy O. de Berker, Robb B. Rutledge, Christoph Mathys, Louise Marshall, Gemma F. Cross, Raymond J. Dolan, and Sven Bestmann, "Computations of Uncertainty Mediate Acute Stress Responses in Humans," *Nature Communications* 7, no. 10996 (2016), https://doi.org/10.1038 /ncomms10996.

13. Barbara Ehrenreich, "Smile! You've Got Cancer," *The Guardian*, January 2, 2010, www.the guardian.com/lifeandstyle/2010/jan/02/cancer-positive-thinking-barbara-ehrenreich.

14. "Gartner Cautions HR Leaders That the Risk of Change Fatigue among Employees Has Doubled in 2020," Gartner.com, October 14, 2020, www.gartner.com/en/newsroom/press-releases /2020-10-14-gartner-cautions-hr-leaders-that-the-risk-of-change-fatigue-among-employees -has-doubled-in-2020-this-year.

15. "Overcoming Disruption in a Distributed World," Asana.com, n.d., https://asana.com /resources/anatomy-of-work.

16. Megan Cerullo, "Nearly 3 Million U.S. Women Have Dropped Out of the Labor Force in the Past Year," CBS News, February 5, 2021, www.cbsnews.com/news/covid-crisis-3-million -women-labor-force.

17. Pooja Lakshmin, "How Society Has Turned Its Back on Mothers," *The New York Times*, February 4, 2021, www.nytimes.com/2021/02/04/parenting/working-mom-burnout-coronavirus.html.

18. Rebecca Solnit, quoted in Maria Popova, "*A Field Guide to Getting Lost*: Rebecca Solnit on How We Find Ourselves," *Brain Pickings*, August 4, 2014, www.brainpickings.org/2014/08 /04/field-guide-to-getting-lost-rebecca-solnit.

19. Sapolsky, *Why Zebras Don't Get Ulcers*, 416.

20. Kate Sweeny, quoted in *Atlantic* Marketing Team, "How Planning for Tomorrow Can Ease Uncertainty Today," *Atlantic Re:think*/Equitable, n.d., www.theatlantic.com/sponsored/equitable -2020/planning-for-tomorrow/3523.

21. Sarah Wilson, *First, We Make the Beast Beautiful: A New Journey through Anxiety* (Sydney, NSW: Pan Macmillan, 2019), 58.

22. Jill Bolte Taylor, *My Stroke of Insight: A Brain Scientist's Personal Journey* (New York: Plume, 2016), 153.
23. Francesca Gino and Michael I. Norton, "Why Rituals Work," *Scientific American*, May 14, 2013, www.scientificamerican.com/article/why-rituals-work.
24. Marielle Segarra, "What Is Makeup for during a Pandemic?," *Marketplace*, Minnesota Public Radio, February 10, 2021, www.marketplace.org/2021/02/10/why-wear-makeup-during -pandemic.
25. Ijeoma Oluo, quoted in Leah Chernikoff, "Why It's Totally Fine to Wear Makeup during a Pandemic," *Time*, April 7, 2020, https://time.com/5816846/coronavirus-makeup.
26. Sharon Salzberg, *Faith: Trusting Your Own Deepest Experience* (London: Element, 2003).
27. Interview with the authors, March 26, 2021.
28. Interview with the authors, April 6, 2021.
29. Interview with the authors, September 30, 2020.
30. Interview with the authors, September 14, 2020.
31. "Headspace: Unwind Your Mind," featuring Andy Puddicombe, Evelyn Lewis Prieto, and Ginger Daniels, 2021, on Netflix, www.netflix.com/title/81328829.
32. Emmy E. Werner, "Resilience in Development," *Current Directions in Psychological Science* 4, no. 3 (June 1, 1995): 81–84, https://doi.org/10.1111/1467-8721.ep10772327.
33. Maria Konnikova, "How People Learn to Become Resilient," *The New Yorker*, February 11, 2016, www.newyorker.com/science/maria-konnikova/the-secret-formula-for-resilience.
34. Interview with the authors, September 20, 2020.

CHAPTER 2: **COMPARISON**

1. Nihar Chhaya, "The Upside of Career Envy," *Harvard Business Review*, June 16, 2020, https://hbr.org/2020/06/the-upside-of-career-envy.
2. Timothy B. Lee, "Study: Lottery Winners' Neighbors Tend to Spend Themselves into Bankruptcy," *Vox*, February 23, 2016, www.vox.com/2016/2/23/11095102/inequality-lottery-bankruptcy-study.
3. Christine Harris, quoted in Nancy Wartik, "Quarantine Envy Got You Down? You're Not Alone," *The New York Times*, August 10, 2020, www.nytimes.com/2020/08/10/smarter-living /quarantine-envy-pandemic.html.
4. Scott L. Feld, "Why Your Friends Have More Friends Than You Do," *American Journal of Sociology* 96, no. 6 (May 1991): 1464–77, https://doi.org/10.1086/229693.
5. Amy Summerville and Neal J. Roese, "Dare to Compare: Fact-Based versus Simulation-Based Comparison in Daily Life," *Journal of Experimental Social Psychology* 44, no. 3 (May 2008): 664–71, https://doi.org/10.1016/j.jesp.2007.04.002.
6. Joanne V. Wood, "What Is Social Comparison and How Should We Study It?," *Personality and Social Psychology Bulletin* 22, no. 5 (1996): 520–37, https://doi.org/10.1177/0146167296225009.
7. Charles Cooley, *Human Nature and the Social Order* (New York: Schocken Books, 1964).
8. Woodruff Health Sciences Center, Adam Galinsky and Maurice Schweitzer, *Friend & Foe: When to Cooperate, When to Compete, and How to Succeed at Both* (New York: Currency, 2015), 21.

9. Interview with the authors, January 17, 2021.
10. Interview with the authors, January 22, 2021.
11. Daniel Kahneman and Amos Tversky, "Prospect Theory: An Analysis of Decision under Risk," chapter 6 of *Handbook of the Fundamentals of Financial Decision Making*, edited by Leonard C. MacLean and William T. Ziemba (World Scientific, 2013), 99–127, https://doi.org/10.1142/9789814417358_0006.
12. Interview with the authors, January 24, 2021.
13. Interview with the authors, January 15, 2021.
14. Aminatou Sow, "Gentle Suggestions," Crème de la Crème, February 3, 2021, https://aminatou.substack.com/p/gentle-suggestions-1db.
15. Abby Govindan (@abbygov), "just found out one of the girls my boyfriend dated before me is pretty.... I'm sick to my stomach," Twitter, June 23, 2021, 12:51 A.M., https://twitter.com/abbygov/status/1407924254516166665.
16. Maria Konnikova, "Can Envy Be Good for You?," *The New Yorker*, August 10, 2015, www.newyorker.com/science/maria-konnikova/can-envy-be-good-for-you.
17. H. W. Van Den Borne, J. F. A. Pruyn, and W. J. A. Van Den Heuvel, "Effects of Contacts between Cancer Patients on Their Psychosocial Problems," *Patient Education and Counseling* 9, no. 1 (February 1987): 33–51, https://doi.org/10.1016/0738-3991(87)90107-8.
18. Johannes Haushofer, "Johannes Haushofer CV of Failures," version accessed September 20, 2021 (n.d.), www.uni-goettingen.de/de/document/download/bed2706fd34e29822004dbe29cd00bb5.pdf/Johannes_Haushofer_CV_of_Failures[1].pdf.
19. Susan Pinker, "The Worst Form of Envy? In the Future Tense," *The Wall Street Journal*, June 14, 2019, www.wsj.com/articles/the-worst-form-of-envy-in-the-future-tense-11560527404.
20. The Newsroom, "Three Quarters of Us Admit to Lying on Social Media," *Hemel Today*, April 24, 2016, www.hemeltoday.co.uk/news/three-quarters-us-admit-lying-social-media-1246364.
21. Mai-Ly Nguyen Steers, quoted in Rebecca Webber, "The Comparison Trap," *Psychology Today*, November 7, 2017, www.psychologytoday.com/intl/articles/201711/the-comparison-trap.
22. Alison Wood Brooks, Karen Huang, Nicole Abi-Esber, Ryan W. Buell, Laura Huang, and Brian Hall, "Mitigating Malicious Envy: Why Successful Individuals Should Reveal Their Failures," *Journal of Experimental Psychology: General* 148, no. 4 (2019): 667–87, https://doi.org/10.1037/xge0000538.
23. Cheryl Strayed, *Brave Enough* (New York: Alfred A. Knopf, 2015), 121.
24. Carrie Kerpen, "Stop Comparing Your Behind-the-Scenes with Everyone's Highlight Reel," *Forbes*, July 29, 2017, www.forbes.com/sites/carriekerpen/2017/07/29/stop-comparing-your-behind-the-scenes-with-everyones-highlight-reel/?sh=72cc8ed03a07.
25. University of Houston, "Facebook Use Linked to Depressive Symptoms," *ScienceDaily*, April 6, 2015, www.sciencedaily.com/releases/2015/04/150406144600.htm.
26. Naomi Fry, "Cazzie David's Existential Dread," *The New Yorker*, November 16, 2020, www.newyorker.com/magazine/2020/11/23/cazzie-davids-existential-dread.
27. James Hamblin, "The Key to Healthy Facebook Use: No Comparing to Other Lives," *The Atlantic*, April 8, 2015, www.theatlantic.com/health/archive/2015/04/ways-to-use-facebook-without-feeling-depressed/389916.
28. University of Houston, "Facebook Use Linked to Depressive Symptoms."

29. Shai Davidai and Sebastian Deri, "The Second Pugilist's Plight: Why People Believe They Are Above Average but Are Not Especially Happy about It," *Journal of Experimental Psychology: General* 148, no. 3 (March 2019): 570–87, https://doi.org/10.1037/xge0000580.

30. Moya Sarner, "The Age of Envy: How to Be Happy When Everyone Else's Life Looks Perfect," *The Guardian*, October 9, 2018, www.theguardian.com/lifeandstyle/2018/oct/09/age-envy-be -happy-everyone-else-perfect-social-media.

31. Sarner, "Age of Envy."

32. Interview with the authors, January 21, 2021.

33. Laura Morgan Roberts, Emily D. Heaphy, and Brianna Barker Caza, "To Become Your Best Self, Study Your Successes," *Harvard Business Review*, May 14, 2019, https://hbr.org/2019/05 /to-become-your-best-self-study-your-successes.

34. Interview with the authors, September 20, 2020.

CHAPTER 3: ANGER

1. Charles Duhigg, "The Real Roots of American Rage," *The Atlantic*, January 3, 2019, www .theatlantic.com/magazine/archive/2019/01/charles-duhigg-american-anger/576424.

2. David Kessler, quoted in Elizabeth Bernstein, "How to Move Forward after Loss," *The Wall Street Journal*, April 6, 2021, www.wsj.com/articles/finding-meaning-as-we-grieve-a-year-of -pandemic-loss-11617724799.

3. Interview with the authors, April 2, 2021.

4. Diana Kwon, "Explaining Rage: A Q&A with R. Douglas Fields," *Scientific American*, March 1, 2016, www.scientificamerican.com/article/explaining-rage-a-q-a-with-r-douglas-fields.

5. Myisha Cherry, "Anger Can Build a Better World," *The Atlantic*, August 25, 2020, www.the atlantic.com/ideas/archive/2020/08/how-anger-can-build-better-world/615625.

6. Audre Lorde, "Uses of Anger," *Black Past*, August 12, 2012, www.blackpast.org/african -american-history/speeches-african-american-history/1981-audre-lorde-uses-anger-women -responding-racism.

7. Augusten Burroughs, *This Is How: Surviving What You Think You Can't* (London: Picador, 2013), 15.

8. Richard A. Fabes and Carol Lynn Martin, "Gender and Age Stereotypes of Emotionality," *Personality and Social Psychology Bulletin* 17, no. 5 (October 1, 1991): 532–40, https://doi.org /10.1177/0146167291175008.

9. Melissa Harris-Perry, "Women Are Angrier Than Ever Before—and They're Doing Something About It," *Elle*, March 9, 2018, www.elle.com/culture/career-politics/a19297903/elle-survey -womens-anger-melissa-harris-perry. *Esquire* Editors, "American Rage: The *Esquire*/NBC News Survey," *Esquire*, January 3, 2016, www.esquire.com/news-politics/a40693/american-rage -nbc-survey.

10. Liz Clarke, "In Her Anger, in Defeat, Serena Williams Starts an Overdue Conversation," *The Washington Post*, September 9, 2018, www.washingtonpost.com/sports/tennis/in-her-anger -in-defeat-serena-williams-starts-an-overdue-conversation/2018/09/09/9d9125ea-b468-11e8 -94eb-3bd52dfe917b_story.html.

11. Marc Berman, "Serena Acted Like a Sore Loser," *New York Post*, September 8, 2018, https:// nypost.com/2018/09/08/serena-acted-like-a-sore-loser.

12. Marc Berman, "Novak Djokovic's Excessive Punishment Is Terrible for US Open," *New York Post*, September 6, 2020, https://nypost.com/2020/09/06/novak-djokovics-disqualification-is-terrible-for-the-us-open. Chandni G, "Why Did We Treat Novak Djokovic So Differently to Serena Williams?," *Upworthy*, September 8, 2020, https://scoop.upworthy.com/why-did-we-treat-novak-djokovic-so-differently-to-serena-williams.

13. Shoshana N. Jarvis and Jason A. Okonofua, "School Deferred: When Bias Affects School Leaders," *Social Psychological and Personality Science*, October 10, 2019, https://journals.sagepub.com/doi/abs/10.1177/1948550619875150.

14. Soraya Chemaly, "Five Myths about Anger," *The Washington Post*, September 14, 2018, www.washingtonpost.com/outlook/five-myths/five-myths-about-anger/2018/09/14/ad457dc8-b7a2-11e8-94eb-3bd52dfe917b_story.html.

15. J. Celeste Walley-Jean, "Debunking the Myth of the 'Angry Black Woman': An Exploration of Anger in Young African American Women," *Black Women, Gender + Families* 3, no. 2 (Fall 2009): 68–86, www.jstor.org/stable/10.5406/blacwomegendfami.3.2.0068.

16. Yuhua Wang, "Asians Are Stereotyped as 'Competent but Cold.' Here's How That Increases Backlash from the Coronavirus Pandemic," *The Washington Post*, May 18, 2020, www.washingtonpost.com/politics/2020/04/06/asians-are-stereotyped-competent-cold-heres-how-that-increases-backlash-coronavirus-pandemic.

17. Nan Ma, "Suspended Subjects: The Politics of Anger in Asian American Literature" (PhD diss., University of California, Riverside, 2009), https://escholarship.org/uc/item/7kx173md.

18. Ah Joo Shin, "'Angry Asian Man' Blogger Talks Stereotypes," *Yale Daily News*, March 21, 2011, https://yaledailynews.com/blog/2011/03/21/angry-asian-man-blogger-talks-stereotypes.

19. Brad J. Bushman, "Does Venting Anger Feed or Extinguish the Flame? Catharsis, Rumination, Distraction, Anger, and Aggressive Responding," *Personality and Social Psychology Bulletin* 28, no. 6 (2002): 724–31, https://doi.org/10.1177/0146167202289002.

20. Chemaly, "Five Myths about Anger."

21. Jason Kornwitz, "Why 'Rage Rooms' Won't Solve Your Anger Issues," *News @ Northeastern*, Northeastern University, August 16, 2017, https://news.northeastern.edu/2017/08/16/why-rage-rooms-wont-solve-your-anger-issues.

22. Bushman, "Does Venting Anger Feed or Extinguish the Flame?"

23. Jeanne Whalen, "Angry Outbursts Really Do Hurt Your Health, Doctors Find," *The Wall Street Journal*, March 23, 2015, www.wsj.com/articles/angry-outbursts-really-do-hurt-your-health-doctors-find-1427150596.

24. Margot Bastin, Patricia Bijttebier, Filip Raes, and Michael W. Vasey, "Brooding and Reflecting in an Interpersonal Context," *Personality and Individual Differences* 63 (June 2014): 100–105, www.sciencedirect.com/science/article/abs/pii/S0191886914000890.

25. Interview with the authors, September 20, 2020.

26. Kelly Conaboy, "Women React to Kavanaugh Hearing with Rage and Pain," *The Cut*, September 27, 2018, www.thecut.com/2018/09/women-react-to-kavanaugh-hearing-on-twitter-sexual-assault.html. Opheli Garcia Lawler, "The Collective Wail of Women," *The Cut*, October 6, 2018, www.thecut.com/2018/10/women-react-to-brett-kavanaughs-supreme-court-confirmation.html.

27. R. Douglas Fields, *Why We Snap: Understanding the Rage Circuit in Your Brain* (New York: Dutton, 2016), 341.
28. Diana Kwon, "*Scientific American MIND* Reviews *Why We Snap*," *Scientific American*, March 1, 2016, www.scientificamerican.com/article/scientific-american-mind-reviews-why-we-snap.
29. Soraya Chemaly, *Rage Becomes Her: The Power of Women's Anger* (New York: Atria Books, 2018).
30. Interview with the authors, June 1, 2021.
31. Elizabeth Bernstein, "The Art of the Pandemic Meltdown," *The Wall Street Journal*, October 6, 2020, www.wsj.com/articles/the-art-of-the-meltdown-11602015018.
32. Tim Heaton, "Heaton: 35 Southern Expressions for Anger," *Hotty Toddy News*, December 10, 2015, www.hottytoddy.com/2015/12/10/heaton-35-southern-expressions-for-anger.
33. Anne Kreamer, *It's Always Personal: Navigating Emotion in the New Workplace* (New York: Random House, 2012).
34. National Institute of Mental Health, "Men and Depression," January 2017, www.nimh.nih.gov/health/publications/men-and-depression.
35. Chemaly, *Rage Becomes Her*, 260.
36. Interview with the authors, July 6, 2021.
37. Emily Shapiro, "Georgia Sheriff's Department under Fire after Official Says Spa Shootings Suspect Had 'Really Bad Day,'" ABC News, March 19, 2021, https://abcnews.go.com/US/georgia-sheriffs-department-fire-official-spa-shootings-suspect/story?id=76533598.
38. Jennifer Li, "Dear Asian American Girls, Let Yourselves Be Angry," *HelloGiggles*, March 19, 2021, https://hellogiggles.com/lifestyle/asian-american-girls-anger.
39. Peter Bregman, "Outsmart Your Next Angry Outburst," *Harvard Business Review*, May 6, 2016, https://hbr.org/2016/05/outsmart-your-next-angry-outburst.
40. Interview with the authors, September 20, 2020.
41. Chris Gilbert, "7 Creative Ways to Express Hot Anger," *Heal the Mind to Heal the Body* (blog), *Psychology Today*, May 19, 2018, www.psychologytoday.com/us/blog/heal-the-mind-heal-the-body/201805/7-creative-ways-express-hot-anger.
42. JR Thorpe, "18 Words for Sadness That Don't Exist in English," *Bustle*, June 29, 2015 (updated February 24, 2020), www.bustle.com/p/18-words-for-sadness-depression-that-dont-exist-in-english-7260841.
43. "Harnessing the Power of 'The Angry Black Woman,'" *All Things Considered*, NPR, February 24, 2019, www.npr.org/2019/02/24/689925868/harnessing-the-power-of-the-angry-black-woman.
44. Lina Perl, quoted in Rebecca Dolgin, "Rage On: A Use Case for Anger," *Psycom*, August 17, 2020, www.psycom.net/rage-anger.
45. Chemaly, "Five Myths about Anger."
46. Cherry, "Anger Can Build a Better World."
47. Anna Chui, "How Can You Transform Your Hulk Anger into Something Good?," *Lifehack*, February 27, 2018, www.lifehack.org/659502/how-can-you-transform-your-hulk-anger-into-something-good.
48. Kwon, "*Scientific American MIND* Reviews *Why We Snap*."

49. Jen-Shou Yang and Ha Viet Hung, "Emotions as Constraining and Facilitating Factors for Creativity: Companionate Love and Anger," *Creativity and Innovation Management* 24, no. 2 (June 2015): 217–30, https://doi.org/10.1111/caim.12089.

50. Adam Grant, "Frustrated at Work? That Might Just Lead to Your Next Breakthrough," *The New York Times*, March 8, 2019, www.nytimes.com/2019/03/08/smarter-living/frustrated-at -work-that-might-just-lead-to-your-next-breakthrough.html.

CHAPTER 4: BURNOUT

1. Grillo, "Jill Soloway Is a 'Weird Girl,'" *Lenny*, March 30, 2018, www.lennyletter.com/story /jill-soloway-is-a-weird-girl.

2. Karlyn Borysenko, "Burnout Is Now an Officially Diagnosable Condition: Here's What You Need to Know about It," *Forbes*, May 29, 2019, www.forbes.com/sites/karlynborysenko/2019 /05/29/burnout-is-now-an-officially-diagnosable-condition-heres-what-you-need-to-know -about-it.

3. "Academy of Work Index 2021: Overcoming Disruption in a Distributed World," Asana, 2021, https://resources.asana.com/rs/784-XZD-582/images/PDF-FY21-Global-EN-Anatomy%20 of%20Work%20Report.pdf.

4. American College Health Association, "ACHA National College Health Assessment Spring 2019 Report," 2019, www.acha.org/documents/ncha/NCHA-II_SPRING_2019_US_REFER ENCE_GROUP_DATA_REPORT.pdf.

5. Da-Yee Jeung, Changsoo Kim, and Sei-Jin Chang, "Emotional Labor and Burnout: A Review of the Literature," *Yonsei Medical Journal* 59, no. 2 (March 1, 2018): 187–93, https://doi.org /10.3349/ymj.2018.59.2.187.

6. Nancy Beauregard, Alain Marchand, Jaunathan Bilodeau, Pierre Durand, Andrée Demers, and Victor Y. Haines III, "Gendered Pathways to Burnout: Results from the SALVEO Study," *Annals of Work Exposures and Health* 62, no. 4 (May 2018): 426–37, https://doi.org/10.1093 /annweh/wxx114. Garret D. Evans, N. Elizabeth Bryant, Julie Sarno Owens, and Kelly Kou- kos, "Ethnic Differences in Burnout, Coping, and Intervention Acceptability among Child- care Professionals," *Child and Youth Care Forum* 33 (October 2004): 349–71, https://doi.org /10.1023/b:ccar.0000043040.54270.dd. Liselotte N. Dyrbye, Matthew R. Thomas, Mashele M. Huschka, Karen L. Lawson, Paul J. Novotny, Jeff A. Sloan, and Tait D. Shanafelt, "A Multi- center Study of Burnout, Depression, and Quality of Life in Minority and Nonminority US Medical Students," *Mayo Clinic Proceedings* 81, no. 11 (November 2006): 1435–42, www .mayoclinicproceedings.org/article/S0025-6196(11)61249-4/fulltext.

7. Kelly Pierre-Louisa, quoted in Brianna Holt, "Beyond Burnout," *The Cut*, August 13, 2020, www.thecut.com/article/black-women-on-burnout.html.

8. Moya Sarner, "How Burnout Became a Sinister and Insidious Epidemic," *The Guardian*, Feb- ruary 21, 2018, www.theguardian.com/society/2018/feb/21/how-burnout-became-a-sinister -and-insidious-epidemic.

9. Dax Shepard, "Day 7," *Armchair Expert with Dax Shepard* (podcast), September 21, 2020, https://armchairexpertpod.com/pods/day-7.

10. Richard Gunderman, "For the Young Doctor about to Burn Out," *The Atlantic*, February 21, 2014, www.theatlantic.com/health/archive/2014/02/for-the-young-doctor-about-to-burn-out/284005.
11. WTOP staff, "Study Finds People Check Email an Average of 74 Times Daily," WTOP News, June 18, 2014, https://wtop.com/news/2014/06/study-finds-people-check-email-an-average-of-74-times-daily.
12. Tara Haelle, "Your 'Surge Capacity' Is Depleted—It's Why You Feel Awful," *Elemental*, Medium, August 17, 2020, https://elemental.medium.com/your-surge-capacity-is-depleted-it-s-why-you-feel-awful-de285d542f4c.
13. Emily Nagoski and Amelia Nagoski, *Burnout: The Secret to Solving the Stress Cycle* (London: Vermilion, 2019).
14. Claudia Canavan, "How to De-stress: Why You Need to Learn How to Complete the 'Stress Cycle,'" *Women's Health*, February 11, 2020, www.womenshealthmag.com/uk/health/mental-health/a27098268/how-to-de-stress.
15. Christina Maslach and Michael P. Leiter, "How to Measure Burnout Accurately and Ethically," *Harvard Business Review*, March 19, 2021, https://hbr.org/2021/03/how-to-measure-burnout-accurately-and-ethically.
16. Maslach and Leiter, "How to Measure Burnout Accurately and Ethically."
17. Mary Bray Pipher, *Seeking Peace: Chronicles of the Worst Buddhist in the World* (New York: Riverhead Books, 2010), 12.
18. Constance Grady, "The Uneasy Intimacy of Work in a Pandemic Year," *Vox*, March 19, 2021, www.vox.com/culture/22308547/pandemic-anniversary-labor-works-intimacy-how-to-do-nothing.
19. Interview with the authors, December 13, 2020.
20. David Sedaris, "Laugh, Kookaburra," *The New Yorker*, August 17, 2009, www.newyorker.com/magazine/2009/08/24/laugh-kookaburra. See also James Clear and Nir Eyal, "The Four Burner Theory for How to Manage Your Ambitions," Next Big Idea Club, https://nextbigideaclub.com/magazine/conversation-four-burner-theory-manage-ambitions/15027.
21. Kaitlyn Greenidge, "The Once & Future Beyoncé," *Harper's Bazaar*, September 2021, www.harpersbazaar.com/culture/features/a37039502/beyonce-evolution-interview-2021.
22. Nagoski and Nagoski, *Burnout*.
23. Nedra Glover Tawwab, *Set Boundaries, Find Peace: A Guide to Reclaiming Yourself* (New York: TarcherPerigee, 2021), xviii.
24. Interview with the authors, July 3, 2021.
25. Ryan Holiday, "33 Things I Stole from People Smarter Than Me," *Forge*, Medium, June 17, 2020, https://forge.medium.com/33-things-i-stole-from-people-smarter-than-me-on-the-way-to-33-c38e368e5cb8.
26. Interview with the authors, September 20, 2021.
27. Connie Wang, "The 'Grateful to Be Here' Generation Has Some Apologizing to Do," *Refinery 29*, June 22, 2020, www.refinery29.com/en-us/2020/06/9867469/working-in-toxic-media-industry-diversity-movement.

28. Yu Tse Heng and Kira Schabram, "Your Burnout Is Unique. Your Recovery Will Be, Too," *Harvard Business Review*, April 19, 2021, https://hbr.org/2021/04/your-burnout-is-unique-your-recovery-will-be-too.

29. Jenna Wortham (@jennydeluxe), Twitter post, March 5, 2021, https://twitter.com/jenny deluxe/status/1367957368315797507.

30. Monique Valcour, "Beating Burnout," *Harvard Business Review*, November 2016, https://hbr.org/2016/11/beating-burnout.

31. Dare Obasanjo (@Carnage4Life), Twitter post, March 30, 2021, https://twitter.com/Carnage4 Life/status/1376943805589413888.

32. Interview with the authors, December 4, 2020.

33. Toni Morrison, "The Work You Do, the Person You Are," *The New Yorker*, May 29, 2017, www.newyorker.com/magazine/2017/06/05/the-work-you-do-the-person-you-are.

34. Janna Koretz, "What Happens When Your Career Becomes Your Whole Identity," *Harvard Business Review*, December 26, 2019, https://hbr.org/2019/12/what-happens-when-your-career-becomes-your-whole-identity.

35. Brené Brown and Scott Sonenshein, "Brené with Scott Sonenshein on Stretching and Chasing," *Unlocking Us with Brené Brown* (podcast), September 9, 2020, https://brenebrown.com/podcast/brene-with-scott-sonenshein-on-stretching-and-chasing/#close-popup.

36. "It's All Quality Time," *Daily Dad*, June 19, 2019, https://dailydad.com/its-all-quality-time.

37. Jonathan Smallwood and Jonathan W. Schooler, "The Science of Mind Wandering: Empirically Navigating the Stream of Consciousness," *Annual Review of Psychology* 66, no. 1 (January 2015): 487–518, https://doi.org/10.1146/annurev-psych-010814-015331.

38. David Goss, quoted in Brad Stulberg, "Sometimes Not Working Is Work, Too," *The Cut*, July 10, 2017, www.thecut.com/article/sometimes-not-working-is-work-too.html.

39. Interviews with the authors, July 2, 2021.

40. Jeremy Bailenson, "Why Zoom Meetings Can Exhaust Us," *The Wall Street Journal*, April 3, 2020, www.wsj.com/articles/why-zoom-meetings-can-exhaust-us-11585953336.

41. Bill Chappell, "Overwork Killed More Than 745,000 People in a Year, WHO Study Finds," NPR, May 17, 2021, www.npr.org/2021/05/17/997462169/thousands-of-people-are-dying-from-working-long-hours-a-new-who-study-finds.

42. Nagoski and Nagoski, *Burnout*.

43. Pema Chödrön, *When Things Fall Apart: Heart Advice for Difficult Times* (Boulder, CO: Shambhala, 2016), 17.

CHAPTER 5: PERFECTIONISM

1. Gordon L. Flett and Paul L. Hewitt, "The Perils of Perfectionism in Sports and Exercise," *Current Directions in Psychological Science* 14, no. 1 (2005): 14–18, https://journals.sagepub.com/doi/10.1111/j.0963-7214.2005.00326.x.

2. Ray Williams, "Why Perfectionism Is So Damaging and What to Do about It," n.d., https://raywilliams.ca/why-perfectionism-is-so-damaging-and-what-to-do-about-it.

3. Jane Adams, "More College Students Seem to Be Majoring in Perfectionism," *The New York Times*, January 18, 2018, www.nytimes.com/2018/01/18/well/family/more-college-students -seem-to-be-majoring-in-perfectionism.html.

4. Thomas Curran and Andrew P. Hill, "Perfectionism Is Increasing over Time: A Meta-Analysis of Birth Cohort Differences from 1989 to 2016," *Psychological Bulletin* 145, no. 4 (2019): 410–29, www.apa.org/pubs/journals/releases/bul-bul0000138.pdf.

5. Thomas Curran and Andrew P. Hill, "How Perfectionism Became a Hidden Epidemic among Young People," *The Conversation*, January 3, 2018, https://theconversation.com/how -perfectionism-became-a-hidden-epidemic-among-young-people-89405.

6. Curran and Hill, "How Perfectionism Became a Hidden Epidemic."

7. Anne Lamott, *Stitches: A Handbook on Meaning, Hope and Repair* (New York: Riverhead Books, 2013), 34.

8. Sharon F. Lambert, W. LaVome Robinson, and Nicholas S. Ialongo, "The Role of Socially Prescribed Perfectionism in the Link between Perceived Racial Discrimination and African American Adolescents' Depressive Symptoms," *Journal of Abnormal Child Psychology* 42 (2014): 577–87, https://doi.org/10.1007/s10802-013-9814-0.

9. Interview with the authors, December 3, 2020.

10. Michael Brustein, quoted in Olga Khazan, "The Problem with Being Perfect," *The Atlantic*, November 5, 2018, www.theatlantic.com/health/archive/2018/11/how-perfectionism-can-be -destructive/574837.

11. Interview with the authors, December 13, 2020.

12. Interview with the authors, December 3, 2020.

13. Interview with the authors, December 5, 2020.

14. Williams, "Why Perfectionism Is So Damaging."

15. Amanda Ruggeri, "The Dangerous Downsides of Perfectionism," BBC, February 21, 2018, www.bbc.com/future/article/20180219-toxic-perfectionism-is-on-the-rise.

16. Interview with the authors, December 12, 2020.

17. Lavinia E. Damian, Joachim Stoeber, Oana Negru-Subtirica, and Adriana Băban, "On the Development of Perfectionism: The Longitudinal Role of Academic Achievement and Academic Efficacy," *Journal of Personality* 85, no. 4 (August 2017): 565–77, https://doi.org /10.1111/jopy.12261.

18. Aurélien Graton and François Ric, "How Guilt Leads to Reparation? Exploring the Processes Underlying the Effects of Guilt," *Motivation and Emotion* 41 (2017): 343–52, https://doi.org /10.1007/s11031-017-9612-z.

19. Brené Brown, *Daring Greatly* (New York: Avery, 2015), 75.

20. Interview with the authors, December 3, 2020.

21. Jessica Pryor, quoted in Khazan, "Problem with Being Perfect."

22. Christina Chwyl, Patricia Chen, and Jamil Zaki, "Beliefs about Self-Compassion: Implications for Coping and Self-Improvement," *Personality and Social Psychology Bulletin* 47, no. 9 (September 2021), https://doi.org/10.1177/0146167220965303.

23. Paul Hewitt, quoted in Christie Aschwanden, "Perfectionism Is Killing Us," *Vox*, December 5, 2019, www.vox.com/the-highlight/2019/11/27/20975989/perfect-mental-health-perfectionism.

24. Aaron J. Nurick, "Good Enough Can Be Great," *Harvard Business Review*, August 12, 2011, https://hbr.org/2011/08/good-enough-can-be-great.

25. Interview with the authors, December 12, 2021.

26. Interview with the authors, December 5, 2021.

27. Interview with the authors, September 20, 2020.

28. Interview with the authors, June 27, 2021.

29. Interview with the authors, December 3, 2020.

30. Interview with the authors, December 8, 2020.

31. Interview with the authors, December 7, 2020.

32. Benedict Carey, "Unhappy? Self-Critical? Maybe You're Just a Perfectionist," *The New York Times*, December 4, 2007, www.nytimes.com/2007/12/04/health/04mind.html.

33. David Robson, "The Four Keys That Could Unlock Procrastination," BBC, January 5, 2021, www.bbc.com/worklife/article/20201222-the-four-keys-that-could-unlock-procrastination.

34. Ellen J. Langer and Alison I. Piper, "The Prevention of Mindlessness," *Journal of Personality and Social Psychology* 53, no. 2 (1987): 280–87, https://doi.org/10.1037/0022-3514.53.2.280.

35. Interview with the authors, September 20, 2020.

36. Interview with the authors, August 3, 2021.

37. Melody Wilding, "Stop Being So Hard on Yourself," *Harvard Business Review*, May 31, 2021, https://hbr.org/2021/05/stop-being-so-hard-on-yourself.

CHAPTER 6: DESPAIR

1. Bruce Bower, "'Deaths of Despair' Are Rising. It's Time to Define Despair," *Science News*, November 2, 2020, www.sciencenews.org/article/deaths-of-despair-depression-mental-health-covid-19-pandemic.

2. William E. Copeland, Lauren Gaydosh, Sherika N. Hill, Jennifer Godwin, Kathleen Mullan Harris, E. Jane Costello, and Lilly Shanahan, "Associations of Despair with Suicidality and Substance Misuse among Young Adults," *JAMA Network Open* 3, no. 6 (June 23, 2020), https://jamanetwork.com/journals/jamanetworkopen/fullarticle/2767515.

3. Bower, "'Deaths of Despair' Are Rising."

4. Shayla Love, "More People Are Feeling Despair and It Might Be Killing Us," *VICE*, April 22, 2019, www.vice.com/en/article/kzmajw/more-people-are-feeling-despair-and-it-might-be-killing-us.

5. Mayo Clinic staff, "Suicide: What to Do When Someone Is Suicidal," Mayo Clinic, January 31, 2018, www.mayoclinic.org/diseases-conditions/suicide/in-depth/suicide/art-20044707.

6. Andrew Solomon, *The Noonday Demon: An Atlas of Depression* (New York: Scribner, 2015), 55.

7. Interview with the authors, September 20, 2020.

8. Lori Gottlieb, *Maybe You Should Talk to Someone: A Therapist, Her Therapist, and Our Lives Revealed* (New York: Houghton Mifflin Harcourt, 2019), 344.

9. David Kessler, quoted in Elizabeth Bernstein, "How to Move Forward after Loss," *The Wall Street Journal*, April 6, 2021, www.wsj.com/articles/finding-meaning-as-we-grieve-a-year-of-pandemic-loss-11617724799.

10. GSnow reply to u/[deleted], "My friend just died. I don't know what to do," Reddit, May 14, 2011, www.reddit.com/r/Assistance/comments/hax0t/my_friend_just_died_i_dont_know_what_to_do/c1u0rx2.

11. Interview with the authors, June 1, 2021.

12. Alan Morinis, *Everyday Holiness: The Jewish Spiritual Path of Mussar* (Boston: Trumpeter Books, 2007).

13. Interview with the authors, January 17, 2021.

14. Molly Flinkman, "Polished Pain," *Coffee+Crumbs*, June 22, 2021, www.coffeeandcrumbs.net/blog/2021/6/22/polished-pain.

15. Summer Luk, "How I Forgave My Parents' Rejection When I Came Out as Transgender," *Teen Vogue*, June 16, 2017, www.teenvogue.com/story/how-i-forgave-my-parents-transgender.

16. Dira M., "Meet Tik Tok content creator Summer Luk," *The Knockturnal*, July 22, 2021, https://theknockturnal.com/exclusive-meet-tik-tok-content-creator-summer-luk-interview.

17. Christine Miserandino, "The Spoon Theory," ButYouDon'tLookSick.com, 2003, https://butyoudontlooksick.com/articles/written-by-christine/the-spoon-theory.

18. Meghan O'Rourke, "What's Wrong with Me?," *The New Yorker*, August 19, 2013, www.newyorker.com/magazine/2013/08/26/whats-wrong-with-me.

19. Glynnis MacNicol, *No One Tells You This: A Memoir* (New York: Simon & Schuster, 2018), 94, 65.

20. Sarah Manguso, *Ongoingness: The End of a Diary* (London: Picador, 2018), 41.

21. Joy Ekuta, "Please Stop Asking Me, 'How Are You Doing?,'" *Medium*, June 2, 2020, https://medium.com/@joyekuta.

22. Interview with the authors, March 28, 2021.

23. Ashleigh Reddy, "A Look into Our History," HellaJuneteenth.com, www.hellajuneteenth.com/juneteenth-history.

24. Joan D. Chittister, *Scarred by Struggle, Transformed by Hope* (Grand Rapids, MI: William B. Eerdmans, 2005), 63.

CHAPTER 7: REGRET

1. Jason G. Goldman, "Why Bronze Medalists Are Happier Than Silver Winners," *Scientific American*, August 9, 2012, https://blogs.scientificamerican.com/thoughtful-animal/why-bronze-medalists-are-happier-than-silver-winners.

2. Anne Lamott, *Stitches: A Handbook on Meaning, Hope and Repair* (New York: Riverhead Books, 2013), 87.

3. Søren Kierkegaard, *Either/Or: A Fragment of Life*, ed. Victor Eremita, trans. Alistair Hannay (London: Penguin Books, 2004; originally published 1843), 54.

4. Susan B. Shimanoff, "Commonly Named Emotions in Everyday Conversations," *Perceptual and Motor Skills* 58, no. 2 (1984): 514, https://doi.org/10.2466/pms.1984.58.2.514.

5. Lila MacLellan, "A New Study on the Psychology of Persistent Regrets Can Teach You How to Live Now," *Quartz at Work*, June 10, 2018, https://qz.com/work/1298110/a-new-study-on-the-psychology-of-persistent-regrets-can-teach-you-how-to-live-now.

6. Giorgio Coricelli, Hugo D. Critchley, Mateus Joffily, John P. O'Doherty, Angela Sirigu, and Raymond J. Dolan, "Regret and Its Avoidance: A Neuroimaging Study of Choice Behavior," *Nature Neuroscience* 8 (September 2005): 1255–62, https://doi.org/10.1038/nn1514.

7. David Whyte, "Ideas for Modern Living: Regret," *The Guardian*, July 25, 2010, www.the guardian.com/lifeandstyle/2010/jul/25/david-whyte-ideas-modern-living-regret.

8. Michael Craig Miller, "Go Ahead, Have Regrets," *Harvard Business Review*, April 6, 2009, https://hbr.org/2009/04/go-ahead-have-regrets.

9. Colleen Saffrey, Amy Summerville, and Neal J. Roese, "Praise for Regret: People Value Regret above Other Negative Emotions," *Motivation and Emotion* 32 (March 2008): 46–54, https://doi.org/10.1007/s11031-008-9082-4.

10. Sugar [Cheryl Strayed], "Dear Sugar, *The Rumpus* Advice Column #71: The Ghost Ship That Didn't Carry Us," *The Rumpus*, April 21, 2011, https://therumpus.net/2011/04/dear-sugar-the-rumpus-advice-column-71-the-ghost-ship-that-didnt-carry-us.

11. Cheryl Strayed, *Brave Enough* (New York: Alfred A. Knopf, 2015), 22.

12. Colin Jost, *A Very Punchable Face: A Memoir* (New York: Crown, 2020), 304.

13. Thomas Gilovich and Victoria Husted Medvec, "The Experience of Regret: What, When, and Why," *Psychological Review* 102, no. 2 (1995): 379–95, https://doi.org/10.1037/0033-295x.102.2.379.

14. Interview with the authors, August 15, 2021.

15. Interview with the authors, December 30, 2020.

16. Interview with the authors, September 20, 2020.

17. Mr. SponsorPants, "Mr. SponsorPants' Guide on How to Not Regret the Past nor Wish to Shut the Door on It," *Mr. SponsorPants* (blog), September 11, 2008, https://mrsponsorpants.type pad.com/mr_sponsorpants/2008/09/mr-sponsorpan-3.html.

18. Alcoholics Anonymous, "The Twelve Steps of Alcoholics Anonymous," August 2016 revision, www.aa.org/assets/en_US/smf-121_en.pdf.

19. Harold S. Kushner, *Nine Essential Things I've Learned about Life* (New York: Anchor Books, 2016), 54.

20. Gilovich and Medvec, "Experience of Regret."

21. Gilovich and Medvec, "Experience of Regret."

22. Interview with the authors, December 31, 2020.

23. Hongmei Gao, Yan Zhang, Fang Wang, Yan Xu, Ying-Yi Hong, and Jiang Jiang, "Regret Causes Ego-Depletion and Finding Benefits in the Regrettable Events Alleviates Ego-Depletion," *Journal of General Psychology* 141, no. 3 (2014): 169–206, https://doi.org/10.1080/00221309.2014.884053.

24. Charles Duhigg, "'We Don't Really Have Language for Telling the Truth about Parenting': Cheryl Strayed Helps a How To! Listener Decide Whether to Have a Baby," *Slate*, October 5, 2019, https://slate.com/human-interest/2019/10/cheryl-strayed-making-decision-have-kids-how-to.html.

25. Augusten Burroughs, *This Is How: Proven Aid in Overcoming Shyness, Molestation, Fatness, Spinsterhood, Grief, Disease, Lushery, Decrepitude & More. For Young and Old Alike* (New York: Picador, 2012), 171–72.

26. Jost, *A Very Punchable Face*, 305.

CONCLUSION

1. Richard Tedeschi and Lawrence Calhoun, "The Posttraumatic Growth Inventory: Measuring the Positive Legacy of Trauma," *Journal of Traumatic Stress*, July 1996, https://pubmed.ncbi.nlm.nih.gov/8827649.
2. Rainer Maria Rilke, Letter VIII, *Letters to a Young Poet*, trans. A. S. Kline, *Poetry in Translation*, www.poetryintranslation.com/PITBR/German/RilkeLetters.php#anchor_Toc58662123.

Index

despair (*cont.*)
  chronic health issues and, 147–48, 151–52,
      156, 165, 169–71, 175–76
  deaths from, 149
  distancing technique and, 162
  and distancing yourself from people who
      don't get it, 167–69
  and empathy versus sympathy, 169
  and focusing on something
      else, 150–51
  and getting through the
      now, 156–58
  grief, *see* grief
  increase in prevalence of, 149
  indicators of, 148–49
  isolation and, 164, 174
  life comparisons and, 151–52
  meaning and, 173–76
  mental health professionals
      and, 151
  myths about, 150–54
  as permanent, 153–54
  and reaching out to people who get it,
      163–65
  resources on, 236–37
  shame around, 151
  small daily intentions
      and, 161–62
  suicidal feelings, *see* suicide
  taking seriously, 150
  trans and nonbinary people
      and, 168
  what to do for others in, 166–67
  working through, 156–75
destruction therapy, 65
Diana, Princess, 167
distancing technique, 162
Djokovic, Novak, 64
Dorsey, Jack, 174
dragging-out regrets, 189,
    194–96
Duhigg, Charles, 202

eating disorders, 126n
Ehrenreich, Barbara, 8
Ekuta, Joy, 173–74
email, 92
emotions, *see* big feelings
empathy, 114, 130, 169, 207
enmeshment, 110
envy, 35, 44–46, 52, 207
  bad days and, 49
  benign, 46, 47
  defined, 35n
  malicious, 46–48, 54
  noticing what you don't envy, 46
  see also comparison

failure, 125, 128, 138–39
Faith (Salzberg), 155
fear(s)
  defined, 5
  of making decisions, 189,
      194–96
  questions and actions and, 23
  specific, translating anxiety
      into, 17–21
  see also anxiety; uncertainty
Fields, R. Douglas, 62, 66
fight-or-flight response, 92–93
Fleabag, 153
Flett, Gordon, 122
Flinkman, Molly, 164
Flourish, 91
Floyd, George, 173
Fortune, 49
Four Burners Theory, 99
future, 6, 8
  see also uncertainty

Gallaher, Laura, 19, 23
garbage time, 111–12
Geisler, Tanya, 38
gender
  anger expression and, 74–75